Prese

Presenting Skills for Thought-Leaders, Vloggers, and Nerds.

By Dr Paul Harrison

Copyright © 2019 Paul Harrison.
All rights reserved.

For Anthony and Christopher

Table of Contents

Introduction, or 'what is this book and who is it for?' 1
1. What is Presenting? 9
2. Dealing with nerves 13
    Why do we get nervous on camera? 14
    One Deep Breath 16
    Nerves top tips 17
    Exercise 2. Dealing with Nerves - Breathing 20
    Square breathing 21
3. Warm-ups 24
    Body warm-ups 24
    Vocal warm-ups 26
    Exercise 3. Vocal Keep Fit 31
4. Posture 35
    Evaluating & Fixing Poor Posture 35
    Posture – Foundation Techniques 36
    Posture – Fine Tuning 40
    Non-Verbal Communication - Gestures 44
    The Three Gesture Sets 45
    In Summary 48
    Exercise 4. Observation of Posture 50
    Exercise 5. Gesture Plan 51

5. Introduction to Camera 53
   Expression 54
   Recording vs Live – what you need to know 57
   Where to look on camera 60
   Walking on Camera 65
   Exercise 6. Putting it all Together Part 1 69
6. Writing Scripts 70
   Exercise 7. Talking to Time 77
7. Working with a Prompt 79
   Reading from a prompt 81
   Exercise 8. Teleprompter practice. 86
8. Interviews 88
   Being Interviewed 88
   Conducting Interviews 92
   Exercise 9. Practice Interview 98
9. Practical Presenting 99
   Working in 'Expert' TV 100
   Agents 104
   The Secret Ingredient 108
   Tics and Habits 110
   Exercise 10. Pulling it all Together Part 2 112
Bonus Chapter: Self-Shooting 114

Choosing a Camera Type 119
Lighting 122
Audio/Sound 126
Microphones 129
Editing 130
Keep It Simple, Stupid (KISS) 132
Final Thoughts 134
Appendices 135
1. Self-Evaluation Sheet 136
2. Sample Script 142

x

Foreword

By Marc Barkman-Astles, BA Dunelm (aka Mr Soup)

In 2010 I began a YouTube channel called Archaeosoup. This was, in part, to 'keep myself sane' while seeking a job in the North East of England during an economic depression but it was also a place to share with the world my love of archaeology. I began with only a Smartphone for filming, editing and uploading videos! Sat on the floor in front of my modest archaeological library, I rested the phone on a cardboard box and began with a series of videos, the 'A-Z of Archaeology'. Over time I learned to frame the shot, to look 'down the lens' and to engage with the audience I imagined were 'just behind the camera'. A guide book would have been incredibly useful! However, in my case, I could not have taught myself to 'face the camera' had I not first been a Viking!

"You're not a real Viking!" a sea of small faces squint at me suspiciously as I welcome the fourth school-group of the day to the Jorvik Viking Centre, York. It is the autumn of 2008 and this exclamation had become a predictable refrain, punctuating my life as surely as the sun rises in the morning! It had been a long, hot day and I held in a sigh at being accused, yet again, of not being approximately 1,200 years old! My hand comes to rest on the axe hanging from my belt and I look down for a moment at the green woollen tunic I am wearing. A little over a year ago I was wearing an entirely different costume.

Suited and booted, with a cape billowing in the summer breeze, I graduated from Durham University with a hard-won First-Class Degree in Archaeology in 2007. I could not have predicted that in a little over 12 months I would be dressed as 'Ulric', facing down a class of children in an underground museum in York but as it turns out that was exactly where I needed to be. You see, I knew a lot about archaeology, and I thought I knew how to share my enthusiasm with others, but I was still an excruciatingly shy young man. Knowledge, it seems, is only half the equation when it comes to speaking confidently, even about a subject you adore… It also takes practice!

Jorvik was a true baptism of fire. Every day I met people from around the world, young and old, all wanting to learn about the Vikings of York and all wanting to be entertained. For each new group who came down those stairs to see the museum and reconstruction of the Coppergate excavations, there was fresh excitement, a wonder at what waited around the next corner - and crucially there was 'a Viking' waiting to greet them…

I suddenly draw my axe and in one motion 'Ulric' has crossed the room to address the challenge. The children step back with widening eyes and a mix of fear and excitement.

"Is this axe real enough for you, boy?" the boy gingerly reaches out to touch the cold steel, nodding with increasing confidence as my grimace melts into a Cheshire-cat grin.

"Well then. Welcome to Jorvik!" I boom with a smile and a slight bow. "Let me tell you about the exciting things you are about to see!"

Reflecting on my time at Jorvik, it is clear that it was an unusual experience - being simultaneously an archaeologist, a re-enactor and an entertainer. I cherish the way it taught me to engage the public confidently, embracing their excitement with patience, authority and a little humour, but not everyone can share my particular career-path. Indeed, not everyone would want to!

Thankfully you hold in your hands, dear reader, a step by step guide to sharing yourself, your knowledge, your opinions and passions. This is a handbook for engaging with the public and creating a platform to communicate effectively. As you embark on the exercises and reflect upon the ideas outlined in this book, I wish you good luck and the confidence that comes with being (for a little while at least) a Viking!

Mark Barkman-Astles. Founder, Archaeosoup

Limit of liability/disclaimer of warranty:

The reader is urged to review and evaluate the information provided in this book and take adequate precautions. Do not undertake these exercises without first consulting a qualified specialist or doctor, especially if you suffer from any condition that may be exacerbated thereby, including but not limited to, blood pressure, heart problems, asthma, or any pulmonary/respiratory conditions.

By following any instructions provided herein, the reader is confirming that they are fit to undertake said activity and cannot hold close-up presenting, Paul Harrison, or any persons or organisations involved in the creation and promotion of this work or derivatives responsible for any losses, harm or injuries resulting from following the materials and techniques described herein. Always consult a physician, doctor, or relevant specialist before undertaking any form of physical exercise, or the warm-ups and breathing exercises described.

Introduction, or 'what is this book and who is it for?'

It started in 2010, in a cluttered room in north London.

Not this book, but rather the need for it. I'd just put in an audition tape for a television show, my first ever such recording. The show itself sounded promising to my naïve young mind – an adventure show based on an 'Indiana Jones' style concept, romping around the world looking for lost places and historical artefacts. This was, as an aspiring archaeologist, PhD candidate, and media-virgin at the time, very much my dream job. I was hungry at the chance to present such a show, but there was one big problem. For all my archaeological knowledge, I had not one iota of an idea how to present on camera! So, naturally, a series of embarrassing and ill-fated audition tapes ensued.

In one such tape (I cringe to admit this in the here and now) I'd let my friend and temporary cinematographer tie me to a chair dressed as Indiana Jones, thinking this would be a 'cool gimmick.' It was in this, less than auspicious camera-debut that I stammered and fumbled my lines, so carefully memorised, and improvised my way to a standstill. Red-faced and drawing a blank I couldn't help but laugh, and my friend did the same.

"Perhaps you're just not cut-out for being on camera" he remarked, only semi-joking.

But what I'd failed to realise was that presenting wasn't about using gimmicks to get noticed. Thankfully, I persevered and discovered that presenting was about two key things: learning to be natural in unnatural situations and being authentically 'you.'

But, crucially, what I also came to understand was that presenting is a *learned skill*, and one that, with the right training, and some diligence, anyone could master.

Be Prepared

The reality of presenting and hosting for camera is that you rarely have the preparation time you need to undergo extensive presenter training when opportunity arises. Often, you'll be hit up with a request and be on camera within the week, certainly for the audition if not the show itself.

With the advent of Skype, the initial casting process now moves quickly. Producers are keen to move the selection process along and pitch the idea as soon as possible, so less time is wasted in the process. As such, they eliminate candidates based on their showreel and early video conference calls, meaning you'll rarely get a chance to prepare for a proper audition where you can 'shine.'

You need a core base of translatable skills that allow you to adapt your presentation to the presenting opportunity quickly and comfortably, with the focus being on relaying what you – and only you – have expert knowledge on, in a way that engages viewers and elucidates your subject matter well enough to secure further bookings.

No Filler

So why a book like this? If you're reading this, then there's a good chance you're considering an appearance on camera, or maybe you've already started branching out into video work and want to improve your skill set. This book aims to close the gap between those trained for screen, and those for whom the screen is an additional occupation, by giving you the tools you need to appear professional, confident and, most importantly, comfortable on camera. I'll also speak a little of my own experiences, where appropriate, in both presenting and production, to help you understand a little bit about the production process and the media world itself.

Most of us are far more familiar with being on video than the pre-smartphone generation, but there is a world of difference between creating amateur content and presenting professionally. When I started out, with no training in presenting or film, the only options available to me were presenting courses aimed at people who wanted to be career presenters. The problem with these courses, good as they might be, is that they focus on a very different demographic, and a different skill-set. Generic presenter courses don't cover many of the specific skills you need as an expert, but they do often insist on teaching skills you'll rarely, if ever need.

For instance, as an on-screen expert you don't necessarily need to know how to juggle in-ear control room feedback whilst hosting a magazine format prime-time entertainment show. As an on-screen expert, it's highly unlikely you'll ever be hosting Dancing with The Stars. You don't need to slap on a fake smile of pearly whites, and you don't need to attend countless auditions for jobs you don't have expertise in.

Say 'Cheese'

I wasted an awful lot of time learning how to be the next Phillip Scofield or Conan O'Brien. I took professional presenter courses aimed at 'career presenters,' because there was no other option available. I took pains to learn how to interpret in-ear feedback, and present in a live studio, dealing with multiple cameras and cutaways. The emphasis that traditional presenting courses placed on these skills convinced me that they were a worthwhile investment of my time and money. However, in nearly a decade on camera I have never been called upon to use those tv-host-specialist skills as an industry expert; they just weren't relevant to me or what I needed to do on camera.

The most useful skills might seem the most basic, but they are often the hardest skills to master without an experienced guide to direct your development. How to talk to camera, how to talk to time, how to use scripts, prompts, cues, etc. These all seem simple things until you begin. And that's why I've written this book, to home in specifically on exactly how to relax, control your breathing, and present with an air of confidence and authority. All the core skills, nothing unnecessary. Nothing you'll spend forever learning only to never use.

What you *do* need to know, is how to represent your field with authority. How to cover topics from a script of your creation. How to make *your* information, which may be quite technical, more appealing and relatable. Of course, there are many areas of crossover and I encourage you to dig further into these after you've finished the exercises in this book. Techniques such as posture, breathing, and voice projection, are life-long skills which you will build over your careers and will serve you well as you go forward in many aspects of your life.

Structure

The book is broken down by category and follows a simple topic-by-chapter structure. The course segments are intended to be viewed in numerical order, however, if you already have presenting experience and want to dive in to a specific chapter, the lessons are self-contained enough for you to do that. I do, however, recommend going through the whole book, whatever your level of experience, because sometimes we miss out on foundational skills which can cause problems further down the line.

It's complimented by additional material including exercises where you can practise and hone your own presenting skill set. Whilst it may be tempting to simply read the book and take notes, the greatest value will be found by engaging with the exercises. You can only get out of the course what you put in. Improvement takes practice, and your skills will develop far more quickly if you film yourself and work through the exercises given.

Remember, as with all mastery, repetition is key.

The Exercises

The first exercise is simple but extremely important, so please don't skip it. It only asks you to shoot a control video, which is simpler than it sounds. It doesn't need to be high-quality – you can shoot it on a phone or webcam – and it certainly doesn't need to be 'good,' so feel free to stutter and stumble your way through it. There's method to this madness, and I promise you'll see why, later in the book. I'm going to encourage you to do this before you read the book or practise any of the other exercises. It's intended to be done without any prior knowledge so that you'll have an honest understanding of your baseline presenting skills. You can go back to it later as a comparative film whilst improving your skill set. It is more valuable to see our imperfections and mistakes honestly, than it is to put off recording the control video and do it after finishing the book. We need that baseline to see how and specifically where our skills are improving and where they may need more work, so try to do it as soon as you get to the exercise, as it should only take a few minutes.

And, Cut!

The mixture of skills and knowledge in this book should give you a comprehensive understanding of the science and art of presenting. Moreover, this knowledge will help you feel more confident both when applying for presenting roles or producing your own content. Whilst this skill set is specifically focused on camera work, certain techniques and technical skills are universal to presenting and should carry over into other fields of public speaking. I've packed as much into the book as possible to get you well on your way, without padding it out with unnecessary clutter.

I've attempted to write the book I wish I could have had when I was starting out. A virtual course that would be available at short notice, that you never need book into, or travel to. A book that prepares you, as an expert, career professional, or thought-leader, to create an inspiring, authoritative camera presence without wasting time on technical studio skills that you'll never use. A book which focuses on universal essentials so that anyone could become a serious contender.

Nine years, several films, documentaries and even some news appearances later, I'm pleased to say that I proved my friend wrong about being on camera. Or rather, I learned how to take my amateur enthusiasm and build a skill set, with nothing but practice. If it worked for me, a stammering lost goofball once tied to a chair dressed as Indiana Jones, it can work for you, too.

Dr Paul Harrison. A different cluttered room. 2019.

Exercise 1. Control

In a scientific experiment, there's usually a thing called a 'control,' which is an unchanged element against which the experimenter compares their findings to look for any significant differences. Basically, a controlled 'before' to compare to 'after.'

In order to track our progress, we're going to record a short video with no preparation, no script, no prompt and, significantly, no warmup. Just be naturally yourself, talk into the camera and just talk for around a minute, (time yourself)

Talk about the following:
- Your name,
- Your occupation or pastime,
- Areas of special interest,
- What you hope to bring to camera that's fresh or interesting about your field.

When you're done, save that video, watch it back and make sure you keep it for comparison purposes later.

1. What is Presenting?

The first time I formally studied presenting there was an actor in the class. As we went around describing who we were and what we did, everyone assumed that the actor, with their bold personality and easy smile, would be a natural presenter. But whilst there are some common elements in presenting and acting, the reality is that they are very different skills, and the actor struggled more than many of the beginners did in that class. Here we'll examine the nature of presenting, highlighting the key differences it has from acting, and you'll see why that is.

First and foremost, as a presenter you're cultivating the skill of being authentically yourself on camera. Let that sink in for a minute.

You're not trying to be another personality, or character, but rather a heightened form of yourself. This may sound obvious, but it's not an easy thing to do this; to be natural, present and engaged, whilst on camera. You may have experienced how unnatural camera work feels if you've ever had a camera thrust into your face unexpectedly.

Being authentic on camera is also extremely important. Yes, it's a performance, but it isn't one you 'wear' so to speak. It comes from your authentic self. The camera is very good at picking up little details about ourselves and even our moods, that we may not think are obvious in real life. Acting, on the other hand, is half a step (or more) removed from the self, and as such, if you're used to acting, presenting can be a challenge. Actors may come across as too 'performance-focused' and seem insincere or inauthentic. There is a sense of intimacy and rapport required of the presenter which actors wouldn't need when immersed in a role. The key is often to tone it down and let the viewer come 'to you.'

This brings us to another consideration, and that's 'size.' Stage and even camera actors can move about, gesticulate wildly, and generally have 'space' to fill and play with. As a presenter your 'space' is limited to the frame (we'll cover framing shortly), and your camera operator will not appreciate you wildly gesticulating or strolling off camera for them to follow (there are exceptions, and we'll come to those, too). Almost all guest spots on camera will be static, as will be interviews and talking heads. As such, depending on the type of shot, you'll have a small space to fill and small movements can seem bigger and exaggerated. The same goes for expressions and volume. So be mindful how much frame you have available to use when you're on camera, and be careful not to move outside it, or move too much within it. Of course, you still need to bring energy to a piece that you present, but this is done in a subtler way than it typically is on stage. You can move your hands to emphasise a point, but don't do it too much else it becomes distracting.

Another, perhaps obvious, difference between acting and presenting is where your focus and eyeline are. As an actor you are taught to never look directly into the lens, as this breaks the fourth wall and the illusion of the world beyond the camera (there are a few exceptions, but the rule still holds).

As a presenter (with few exceptions that we'll cover in more detail elsewhere) you'll be taught to always look straight into the lens and address the audience. This is where you'll need to develop your 'conversational tone' and make the audience feel like you're addressing them, rather than performing regardless of them.

Rehearsal time and scripts are another obvious major difference between presenting and acting. As an actor, particularly a stage actor, you'll often have weeks or even months to rehearse and learn a script. In television the turnaround is somewhat faster, but generally you'll get a script in advance (even if only a day in advance). So-called sight-reading and improvisation are exceptions, and if you have these skills, you'll find them invaluable as a presenter! For the most part, a presenter has little time with a script, and often doesn't even have one. Unlike actors, if there is a script present it can often be found on a prompt device, such as an autocue or teleprompter (don't worry, we'll cover these, too!).

However, there are plenty of commonalities between acting and presenting; In order to deliver a solid performance, both have to learn how to control breathing, and posture; Clarity of diction and enunciation is important to most presenters and actors (with some obvious exceptions); Being able to harness the power of the voice to confer tone and authority is another transferable skill.

Other technical considerations, from working on a set, being able to hit a mark, and deciphering scripts and jargon from the media industry also have some overlaps, though presenting has many of its own standards and procedures.

2. Dealing with nerves

It's said that the average person fears speaking in public more than death. It's estimated that a whopping 75% of people suffer from a form of anxiety or panic when speaking in public. Worse yet, this fear often extends to all kinds of presentations, including meetings, speeches, and camera work (aka 'stage-fright'). It manifests in the arenas where it counts the most – work, college, oral exams, and especially on camera and in studios.

Facing the camera for the first time isn't as alien as it once might have been. Now that everybody carries a camera around in the form of their phones, most people are a little more used to having a lens shoved in their faces. However, stepping into a studio for a professional shoot, or even recording in your own house for your new business venture, can evoke a very different set of reactions to the playful way we interact with cameras for fun.

The first time I stepped onto a set to record a professional piece, it was terrifying. I got caught up in my own head, I jumbled my lines, and worst of all, I stopped and looked directly at the crew off camera and apologised whilst the cameras were still rolling. Now, this happens to a lot of people, so don't worry, your time may yet come, but I'm going to prepare you with advice I wish I'd had before I first stepped out in front of a camera.

Why do we get nervous on camera?

When we feel threatened or anxious about something, our bodies go into something called 'fight or flight.' This is a function of the nervous system and is completely harmless and even normal. Our nervous system is composed of two parts; the *para*sympathetic nervous system, also known as 'rest and digest' is the state of relaxation we associate with safety and calm, it slows us down, like a *para*chute, (I remember the difference with this 'para' analogy). The *sympathetic* nervous system is the fight or flight aspect, and it releases compounds which prepare us for those activities. The problem is that our bodies don't tend to discern very well between different levels of threat, so when the idea of something usually harmless bothers us (like the fear of public embarrassment), our nervous system can go into overdrive. This is an unfortunate remnant of our hunter-gatherer days, when being stared at like prey, or exiled from the group, could be life-threatening. We subsequently experience unpleasant symptoms (butterflies, rapid heart, shallow breathing) which can send us into a panic loop and exacerbate those symptoms or create even more unpleasantness. Our primitive 'lizard brain' assumes that because our bodies are reacting this way, that something must be physically wrong, or dangerous, and we end up falling apart, forgetting our lines and being unable to speak properly. Worse yet, we rehearse failing in our minds, creating 'worst case scenarios.' We fear we'll be unable to perform, and it's this 'fear of fear' that we get caught up on, indulging our brains in a never-ending cycle of painful fantasy. Our rational minds tell us that rehearsing our way through the worst-case scenario will prepare us, but this behaviour does the opposite, disconnecting us from the present and creating a self-fulfilling prophecy of bad performance.

But here's the good news. Understanding the processes and symptoms that result from nerves and panic can help us overcome them. Once we can identify these, we can learn how to undo our automatic panic responses and reclaim control! We'll do this in three stages –
- Recognition – raising awareness of our nervous system's responses and identifying anxiety triggers.
- Interruption – utilising both physical and psychological methods to stop the cycle in its tracks.
- Control – recognition and interruption will gradually increase our capacity to tolerate, adapt and even harness anxiety and nervous energy.

I'd like you to make a list of the symptoms that you feel when you're speaking in public or on camera, so that you can learn to recognise the moment they begin to happen. This can include anything from a dry mouth, nervous energy, stuttering, short shallow breathing, and even upset stomachs. Once you've recognised these symptoms, we'll start slowly with the first stage of interruption.

One Deep Breath

Everyone can remember this, and it's the first, simplest and most powerful way to take back control as we prepare to give a speech or presentation. **Taking one deep abdominal breath in and out signals the brain that we're engaging the parasympathetic nervous system**, that's to say, the rest and digest system, as opposed to the fight or flight system.

From there, it becomes far easier to manage our mental and emotional, and subsequent behavioural responses. How can taking one breath be so powerful? It comes down to the mind-body connection.

Simply put, the nerves that carry the signals to the parasympathetic and sympathetic nervous systems reside in different parts of the body. By actively engaging the nerves that connect to the parasympathetic nervous system, we remind the body to balance out the effects of anxiety and rein in our panic responses.

Following from this is the revelation that the nervous system is a *two-way street*. We can actively *influence* our nervous system, despite its normally automatic role. We can do this by stimulating the areas that play a role in the parasympathetic nervous system and controlling our breathing to reduce heart rate.

The parasympathetic system is composed of craniosacral nerves, which control many of the muscles in our faces, throats, stomachs, and groin. When the sympathetic system activates, producing compounds which elicit the stress response, many of the processes of the parasympathetic system are put on hold. Basically, our bodies are saying "deal with this threat now and you can digest your lunch later!" (this is why anxiety and stomach problems are often intertwined). However, because the nervous system is a two-way street, we can use breathing, posture and vocal exercises to stimulate these craniosacral nerves and interrupt the panic loop, taking back control of our minds and bodies!

Nerves top tips

Nerves are often the biggest hurdle to a good performance, and the biggest obstacle most people face, so it's important to face them head on and address them early. It's true that the more you practice, even at home, the less likely you'll be plagued by nerves, but a little anxiety is normal when stepping into a new environment, especially a tv studio when you must perform live.

First, some reassurance - In the age of digital recording, now more than ever, it's easy to do additional takes, and directors often secure several takes for good measure. As an expert, it's rare that you'll be asked to perform live, but when it does happen it's good to have a preparatory ritual or routine in place to help you feel cool, calm and collected. Just remember these 5 key tips –

1. Don't try to be perfect – mistakes happen, it's natural, you're human, your viewer understands that. If you make a mistake just move on.

2. Stress in small amounts can be a performance *enhancer*: some nerves are bound to slip through into performance, especially when you're new to presenting. Try to learn how to reframe these as excitement! Use your nervous energy to enrich your performance with more passion! Being nervous whilst presenting is normal and becomes manageable over time. So, accept the nerves and don't let them pull you into a panic state.

3. A little preparation can go a long way. If you have a script, try getting some time before you shoot to go back over the main points. We'll cover script prep later, but for now just remember to take some time before the shoot, as the more prepared you are, the more confident you'll feel, and the less likely it is that nerves will appear in the first place.

4. Picturing yourself as calm and confident as you do your breathing exercises will help achieve that goal. Sometimes, picturing the traits you aspire to, or a personal hero of yours, can invoke those traits within you. Try visualisation exercises before you present, picturing yourself as calm and confident, enjoying your presentation.

5. Practice, practice, practice! You can form a solid foundation of familiarity and confidence by practising your delivery in front of the mirror for three days. then

move on to recording yourself and watching it back. This will help iron out any behavioural tics you might have. Now you're ready to take it to an audience. Start with a small test audience if you can, such as friends or family. This will help limit your nervous response whilst still being a practical run-through for facing a live audience.

Head to the appendix now and try Exercise 10.2, which describes some additional techniques to help you calm your nerves. If you follow these steps before each performance, you'll find that facing an audience or camera soon becomes second nature, and even if nerves still surface, you'll be prepared to mitigate their effects. Eventually, it will become second nature to harness your nervous energy.

Exercise 2. Dealing with Nerves - Breathing

Important: Breathing exercises can cause dizziness and light-headedness. Always do breathing exercises somewhere safe, where you can sit or lay down if necessary. Avoid doing breathing exercises before undertaking intense physical activity. Always consult your doctor or health specialist before undertaking exercise. Only undertake these exercises once you have read and understood all accompanying health warnings.

The best solution to a problem is never having one, so to that end let's go through a beginner technique that you can use to relax and ground yourself before stepping into frame.

The foundation of good performance is in breathing and posture. As luck would have it, breath work not only enhances your performance, but also helps alleviate nerves. It's the effects of shallow breathing, breathing lightly in the chest, that contribute to anxiety and panic, and take the body into fight or flight mode. The common denominator of most of these breathing techniques is that we need to breathe with our *stomachs*, deeply, and slowly. This helps reassure the brain that we are safe and makes us feel calmer.

To ensure that you're breathing correctly, place your hands on your lower abdomen, just below the bellybutton. Try it now. As you breathe in, feel your abdomen expand. All the movement should be in your belly and abdomen. It's an in and out motion, and there should be no up and down movement in the chest and shoulders. It's important to keep your abs relaxed as you breathe as this allows for more vocal power when you need it later.

Sit or lay down somewhere comfortable and just focus on breathing in for four seconds as deeply as you can. Now release the breath slowly. Try to make sure the chest doesn't cave in at any point, as you don't want to be rounding your body inwards. Try this deep in and out breath five times and you should notice a difference. Ten repetitions will make a marked difference. The significance of this simple act cannot be overstated, as you've just consciously activated your parasympathetic nervous system and taken the first step in taking control over nerves!

Practised regularly, breathing is not only good for calming the nerves, but it will also play a major role in our vocal technique, as it provides strength, resilience and power for our vocal chords.

There are several techniques available aimed at reducing anxiety. Below we're going to focus on a practical exercise, which you can do in just a few minutes almost anywhere, even as you compose yourself whilst waiting for the camera to be framed.

Square breathing

Square or box breathing is a technique that's quickly become a go-to for dealing with anxiety and panic, but it's also perfect as part of your warm up routine, and this is something I'll be encouraging you to do before every camera performance.

Find a place to sit down. This can be a chair, or on the floor against a wall, basically anywhere with some back support so that you can sit up straight.

Place your hands on your lap or relaxed at your sides. Try to let go of the tension in your legs and feet, followed by your stomach, chest, arms, hands and finally, your head.

Take a deep breath in and focus on relaxing as you breathe out.

If possible, close your eyes. You can do this with your eyes open, but ideally, you'd have them closed to avoid distractions.

1. Inhale deeply, through the nose if possible, breathing from your stomach, for four seconds.
2. Hold the breath in for four seconds. Let the air fill your lungs. Concentrate on the sensation of the air in your body.
3. Exhale through the mouth for a count of four. Feel the breath leaving completely.
4. Hold the exhale for a further four seconds.

And repeat from the beginning.

Ideally you will do at least one minute of this exercise, but just a few rounds can make a huge difference to your state of calm.

Some variations are available, which may help when you're on the verge of full-blown panic. Find a place to sit and relax as above, but breath in for four seconds, hold for two seconds and breathe out *for six seconds*. A few rounds of this variation actually lowers blood oxygen (so be careful not to do it for too long, or before intense physical activity) – lowering blood oxygen can stop your brain from over-firing when you're on the verge of full-blown panic or an anxiety attack. But use this sparingly as it can cause dizziness.

3. Warm-ups

You don't always have time for a thorough warm-up in a studio right before you go on camera, but increasingly, as we shoot from home, or as we travel, we're on our own schedule.

A warmup does two things. It prepares you physically for the task ahead, by getting the body nice and loose, and the face and jaw relaxed for better speaking. It also prepares you psychologically, it helps alleviate anxiety and nerves, and gets your blood pumping so you naturally feel more psyched and energetic.

If you can't do all these exercises for any reason, don't worry, just do what you can. I'd like to take this opportunity to state that, in the spirit of my motto that anyone can present, feel free to adapt these warm ups should you have any conditions or impairments – if you use a wheelchair, or have back problems, feel free to adapt anything you read in here to your needs. The key factors are balance (even when sitting), space in the torso for adequate breath, and awareness of your posture. With these key components in mind, you can begin to make adjustments that work for you.

Body warm-ups

Now it's time to warm up the body. Don't worry, you don't need to be a yoga-master for any of these exercises, they're composed of simple stretches and basic alignment moves.

Stand with feet shoulder width apart.

Take a couple of breaths to get ready.

First, we're going to start at the bottom, so, try a few calf-raises to get your leg muscles warmed up, just do as many as you can, up to about ten, if you can manage that.

Next, we'll just gently rock the waist and warm up those hips – I want you to do whatever feels the most natural and comfortable for you, don't do anything that will cause pain or excessive strain – I personally am quite fond of rotating a small semicircle with my waist, just around the front, as it engages the core a little.

From here just try some light chest stretches, moving the arms horizontally and outwards.

Moving up the body still, we're going to turn our attention to the shoulders, so start with a few simple shoulder shrugs.

Now, with arms down at our sides, we're going to just roll those shoulders back about 8 times, and forwards about 8 times.

Lift your arms up to the sides, so they're parallel with the floor, and just rotate the tips of your fingers in small circles forwards a few times and backwards a few times. Do this gently, creating little circles with your hands, forwards and backwards, for as long as is comfortable.

Now we'll gently dip the head from side to side, so that your ear moves down towards your shoulder. You should start to feel a slight stretch going all the way from the neck up to the bottom of the jaw – you're letting the ear drop towards the shoulder as far as it remains comfortable.

Bring your head back to the centre for some light head turns, looking 90 degrees left then turning back to the right, looking out over both shoulders - about half a dozen of those usually works.

Finally, now some elements are warmed up, try a whole body stretch, in whatever form you feel most comfortable.

So now that your body is a little warmer, let's move on to the head and jaw!

Vocal warm-ups

Always remember to be mindful of your breathing when doing your warmups, <u>and don't do them at maximum volume.</u> 50 to 75% is usually more than enough. Also, stay hydrated! Good hydration is essential to vocal health, so avoid milk and substances that can dry out the throat, like excessive smoking. If you do smoke, try waiting until after you present, rather than just before you go on, if possible.

We'll start off by gently rubbing the jaw line area. Particularly up under the ears and on the joint of the bone, gently though, you don't want to create too many red marks.

Next, we want to warm up the root of the tongue. Keeping your lips sealed, push your tongue forward so it's past your teeth (but still in your mouth behind your closed lips). Now rotate it full in circles clockwise then anti-clockwise, around seven times each way.

Another quite useful technique is something a speech therapist friend taught me, which is to just place a couple of the fingers and the thumb of one hand on the throat area, either side of the Adam's apple for the gents, about the mid-point where you feel the glands for the ladies. Very gently, lightly massage this area. If you do this for about a minute, you'll notice almost immediately that your vocal register drops, as your throat is warmer and more relaxed. Not everyone likes the sensation, however, so we'll cover some more traditional warm-ups now.

As a first step, try yawning, or if you can't yawn on demand, just imitate the motion of it. Yawning is a very good way of initially opening the jaw and loosening it up, so do that a few times.

Humming – Now we start humming in a low key and moving the sound so that we can feel a vibration in our lips. Just one note is fine.

Pitch – now we take it up in pitch. Take a breath and hold a pitch until you're out of air.

Now move up another pitch, and don't worry, you don't need to be able to sing, it doesn't matter if you're in tune at all.

Trilling – since we're still focused on the lips, we're going to do some trilling – trilling is embarrassing, but almost all presenters and actors do this exercise at some point, so just go with it, it's a great ice-breaker, and something I always enjoy doing with new presenters who are a little nervous as it's a great ice breaker! You start with a high note, and basically blow through your lips as if you were a horse, - and you take the note down through half a scale (or a few notes if music isn't your thing). The goal is to get your mouth as loose as possible, ridiculous as that sounds. Do this at least four times. There are many examples of trilling on YouTube if you need some examples.

Vowels – Now we get into diction and vowel sounds. As a warm up, we'll keep it basic, but I'll include some exercises for both diction and vocal power later. We'll start by going through vowel sounds, that's A E I O U, but overemphasising the sound in order to make as much use of the mouth as possible – speak these aloud as clearly as possible and over-emphasize each sound,

    A
    E
    I
    O
    U

You should really feel that in the jaw, just under the ears, so let's try that again

    A
    E
    I (open wide)
    O
    U

You should move the whole mouth, so that's it's really quite ridiculous.

Now we're going to do a variation of the same thing but we're going to push the tips of our tongues into the roof of the mouth so it's touching the top of the inside of the mouth.

Now as we make the vowel sounds, they should come out quite nasally,

A
E
I
O
U

One more time
A
E
I
O
U

Ok, now your jaw and tongue are starting to warm up and you should feel looser and more pliable.

Lastly, we're going to going to do a few tongue twisters to really refine that diction. Try the following tongue-twister, over-emphasising each sound,

The presenter protested that trilling was embarrassing!

Make sure you hit the end sounds, and just to emphasise that we'll do the same tongue twister but really pull out the vowels and consonants...

Theee preesenterrrr proootesssted thaat triilliiing waas embaaaarrassiiiiing!

A few tongue twisters thrown into your warm up can make a huge difference to your diction, and we'll cover some more in the following exercises.

Exercise 3. Vocal Keep Fit

When you're a presenter it's important to develop your voice and diction as much as any of your other skills. I have a terrible habit of mumbling when I'm not on camera, but I've managed to overcome that habit when on camera by keeping a few basic principles in mind and practising the following exercises.

Remember to use your mouth fully for exercises, this means opening the mouth more than we might in regular speech. I like to throw at least a couple of the following exercises into my warm up regimen, as it takes me longer to prepare my voice for speaking than it does most people, as I had already picked up several bad habits in my youth. These are something you might practice at least twice a week to keep your voice strong.

The first thing we do here is *cough,* very gently, we don't want to strain the throat or the vocal cords. Coughing engages exactly the right parts of the core muscles which we use when we are projecting our speech. So, this reminds us where we're aiming to pull our voice from. Just like with breathing, you don't want to be stuck and tight up in the throat, with your shoulders bunched up, or breathing and talking from your chest.

Ideally, you'll be nice and relaxed post warmup, pulling your breath into a nice relaxed tummy, and projecting the voice from the same place. Notice how much richer and deeper your voice is when you pull from the lower abdomen and *relax the throat and chest*. Also, keep to a relatively low volume as you begin. Don't try to belt with these exercises, or you'll end up with throat strain.

Vocal Strength
These are some techniques that strengthen the jaw and help us develop more powerful vocal range. Start by opening the mouth and putting a finger on your chin, to stop the jaw moving.

Now practise trying to say the following, *without moving the jaw*, keeping your chin as still as possible -

LA GA LA GA LA GA LA GA LAAAAAAA

Next, we're going to put our tongues, so the tip is touching the roof of our mouths like we did in warm up, but now we're going to try to make a *ta ya* sound, like so

ta ya ta ya ta ya ta ya taaaaaaaaa

Remember, do not strain or attempt to produce volume or you'll hurt your throat. 50% volume maximum! Now try a scale of this, moving up through your natural register without straining.

Accents
Even if you have an accent (like I did, originating from east London), you should be aiming not to dampen your accent, so much as make your speech as clear as possible whilst

honouring your natural voice. This is the trick about diction – it doesn't matter if you have a regional or strong accent if your speech is clear and understandable to the viewer. To this end, focus on the following sounds and always aim to hit the ending of words properly. Try this tongue twister a few times. Notice how we differentiate between the t h 'th' sounds and the f 'f' sounds.

When Thor was Four He Fought with Thought and Valour

Now we'll differentiate between the *th* and *v* sounds -

Another lover's brother hovered and bothered the other.

Notice how one th makes a sound at the top near the teeth and the 'v' sound comes from the sides of the mouth with almost an overbite accompanying it

"Am I bo*th*ered?" Vs "Am I bo*vv*ered?"

Here's a few more that might help point out where vocal delivery needs work –

Enough rough fluff is tough to buff enough

The girls at the well quell bells with hurled shells

Notice the different sounds that your mouth is forced to make and focus on those sounds that you find challenging by recording yourself and listening back to the results. Remember always work your weaknesses the hardest when it comes to diction. If you struggle with 'th' sounds or drop the endings of words, concentrate on tongue twisters that challenge these habits and try to stay mindful in day-to-day conversations.

4. Posture

We can use an obvious image here and think of posture as the 'backbone' of good presenting technique. Good posture is a foundation against which all our other skills rest, such as correct breathing, and vocal delivery. It also has the benefit of making us look, and in turn, feel, more confident, authoritative and powerful.

Evaluating & Fixing Poor Posture

It's time to look at our on-screen posture. Why do we worry about posture? Well, in addition to the above, posture is a form of non-verbal communication (nvc), which signals our audience as to who we are. The first impression of a person is evaluated very quickly, (in just 7 seconds!) so we've often been judged before we even open our mouths to speak! For the presenter this makes posture CRUCIAL, as it's the basis of our body language, and the trust or empathy our audience will feel towards us.

There are unconscious signals that we send out with our bodies and faces all the time. Crossed arms and even hands indicate defensiveness, as do hunched shoulders and downward facing heads.

Such non-verbal signals are picked up subconsciously, so we need to know objectively what kind of position we're starting from. You can do this by looking at your natural posture in pictures, where you've been caught unaware and haven't had time to pose. Do you slouch? I know I do. Perhaps you have chronic back pain or sore shoulders, and this has resulted in compensatory movements. Get somebody to take a picture of you standing or sitting naturally, or if alone, stand in front of a mirror but *turn off your mirror pose*. Let yourself relax into your regular way of standing, or sitting as if you're just in the kitchen, making tea, not thinking about it too much.

Ok hold that pose and try to observe objectively – what do you see? I have a habit of letting my mid and lower back relax, which slumps me forward onto my stomach, and pushes the tummy out. Many people stand or sit like this, particularly when in an office chair.

Now the natural reaction to seeing our slovenly selves might be to overcompensate by going stiff or rigid and trying to stand super straight like it's a 1940s army movie…well, that's not necessary, or even helpful. So, let's break down these steps and explore the reasoning behind posture and body language on camera.

Posture – Foundation Techniques

Some people study the Alexander technique to correct poor posture, which helps fix things like rounded shoulders, slouching, stooping and protruding necks.

Teaching the Alexander technique is outside the remit and scope of this course, and I would never claim to be a master of it, but we'll touch on a few on the principles now, and use them as a base from which to work on our posture.

The three key notions are observation, inhibition and direction. Let's unpack that a bit.

1. Observation
   Observation is a mindfulness of our posture. Where the weight rests when we sit or stand, how balanced we are on each side of the body, where we are maybe slouching or holding ourselves in a less than ideal way.
2. Inhibition
   Inhibition means holding back from bad habits but using an appropriate level of effort. i.e. not going too stiff and making things worse!
3. Direction
   Direction is the process of sending specific instructions or thoughts to the body to encourage space and blood flow rather than contraction and tension. This is all managed by the relationship between the head, neck and spine.

The fight or flight response covered in our section on nerves is highly relevant to any discussion of posture. As a defensive mechanism when we're nervous, we compress ourselves and shrink into our bodies. This contraction robs our performance of energy and enthusiasm, because it steals oxygen and movement from the body. Perhaps most importantly, it's uncomfortable to watch.

How do we counter this? Well, for starters, we build space into our bodies from the ground up. So, let's all stand if you can or sit attentively if you can't stand.

Notice the balance of your feet. We all tend to favour one foot and even one cheek of our behinds when sitting ... but try to spread your weight over both. Try anchoring your feet in on your heels and the toes, particularly the big toe and little toe. This 'tripod effect' grounds us and grants stability. I like to call these 'anchor points' which encourage you to feel connected to the ground, or chair, and settled in.

Next move up the body by relaxing the legs up to the knees and letting the kneecaps unclench and float. Feel the mobility but try not to sway.

Now the hips.

The hip joint is quite low, and we want to relax and create space here and correct any problems. We're often told to tuck our bums under by tilting the pelvis forwards, but, whilst this isn't strictly speaking Alexander technique, there's emerging research which suggest that a j shaped back is better for our posture, so I'd advise doing whichever feels and looks most comfortable to you, that you can sustain without difficulty or strain.

The most important areas to the camera tend to be up in the torso.

The tummy needs to be relaxed, not tensed or pulled in. Contracted abdominal muscles only provide power on the moment they are tensed, so in order to power our voices without vocal strain, we want a nice relaxed stomach that we can fill when we breathe in, so it can provide an even flow of air for our vocal chords. Allow the torso to lengthen naturally.

The chest wants to be open, shoulders rolled comfortably back and released out to the sides, so they're almost floating.

The head and neck are the source of a great deal of problems, not just for presenters. I'm sure we've all had sore necks and stiffness, particularly when stressed.

The problem tends to be one of alignment, be it 'chicken neck', or imbalance further down in the spine. This is exacerbated by the weight of the head, which weighs around 15 pounds!

Try to release the neck by gently unrolling the top of the spine from between the shoulder blades to the point between your ears where the spine ends, all the way up where the spine meets the skull. Pull your head back over your body where you should literally feel the weight drop off your shoulders as the spine takes the load.

Just experiment until you can hardly feel the weight of your skull on your shoulders. Proper alignment will have your eyes looking directly into the lens with very little tilt (assuming the camera is set up at eye level!)

Now take a deep breath in.

You should notice that it feels like there's much more space for that air to go now.

A big advantage of this technique is that there's much more air and power available for voice production, and you shouldn't find yourself gasping or stopping as often, due to the nice big reserves of air you've made space for in the body.

So, as you can hopefully see, posture isn't just about looking correct on camera, or in life, but it's also an extremely powerful technique which facilitates vocal power and imbues us with confidence and an air of authority.

Feel free to investigate some more tips on Alexander Techniques or take a class, as it's a transferrable life-skill which will aid you in presenting and in life.

Posture – Fine Tuning

We've covered the foundational basics of posture but let's look at fine-tuning with some commentary on posture more generally, facing, and, importantly, hand gestures and how to use them to maximum effect.

Anchoring in

The first two big no-noes of on-screen presenting are slouching and swaying. If you're putting the posture foundational techniques into practice there won't be any slouching happening, but it's always worth being mindful as some of us, me, in this instance, have a natural tendency to slouch and sometimes we revert to this default setting.

Slouching looks terrible on camera, it looks lazy, it implies a lack of interest in the subject and the audience. Even worse, if sitting, slouching or leaning back can imply arrogance. It also makes our clothes crumble, which is never a good look! It's important to drill in and remember our key points from posture – 1 observation of the body, 2 inhibition of bad habits, 3 direction from your brain for appropriate adjustments.

Another issue stemming from posture is swaying. Swaying is the result of a bad cocktail of uneven posture and nervous energy. When weight isn't properly distributed, it looks strange on screen, but swaying is an absolute no-no on camera!

Any movement on camera is exaggerated greatly by the frame we're placed in. There are three fixes for this –

(1) first is the prep work we did to calm the nerves and relax the nervous energy. Even if there's a little bit of nerves left, preparation can take the edge off enough to stop us fidgeting.

(2) The second thing we can adjust is weight distribution. Remember, anchor in to the floor, or the seat if you're sitting. Make sure you're really embedded in, like a tree with roots going down into the earth. Now relax. Maintain that posture but relax into that position so you don't feel the need to shift uncomfortably. It will come with practice.

(3) The third thing we can do is breathing, as covered in our section on nerves, and believe me, breathing makes all the difference when dealing with pre-performance nerves. Slow, deep stomach-breaths will help you calm that urge to fidget.

Facing

You may have seen instructional videos that advise you to stand at an angle or use a t-stance to stop from swaying side to side. DON'T DO THIS! Standing at an angle to the audience may be more flattering to your profile or not, but it instantly creates a *disconnect* between speaker and viewer, as you are no longer facing them. Subconsciously, we trust a person *more* if we can see their body and hands clearly, head on. Standing side-on prevents this. A side-stance also unbalances your body, restricts airflow, and will strain your neck and throat over longer periods. There are far better ways to avoid swaying, than to stand in a t-formation. As a rule, never stand at an angle or side-on to the camera or audience, and especially, never turn your back on them.

However, when we stand square to a person it conveys interest and engagement, and that's your primary goal when presenting, not just on camera, but to any audience. So square-up, look straight ahead, and engage. The exception, and there's always one, is if you're co-presenting or interviewing, in which case it's more acceptable to sit or stand at an angle so that you face each-other *and* the audience.

Sitting

Sitting creates its own set of issues that must be addressed. As mentioned, slouching is a no-no, so make sure that your posture remains on point! Remember not to swivel or rock and keep a consistent distance from the camera lens. Avoid jogging knees and fidgety energy by anchoring into your chair, as you would when standing. Really feel yourself sink down whilst keeping your posture correct, and take a few breaths to settle in.

One of the most important factors which determines how you sit, is where you place your posterior. If you shift towards the back of the seat, you should be able to rest your back comfortably on the support without leaning too far back. If you sit on the edge of your seat, you'll appear more engaged, but you'll have to support yourself or lean in, which can cause issues with breathing if you're not mindful. Leaning in can be helpful when interviewing or emphasising a point, or when displaying an item. Adapt as the situation demands, and just remember the principles of alignment we discussed in the last section.

Non-Verbal Communication - Gestures

Body language and gestures are extremely powerful non-verbal communicators, and even on screen, we are communicating as much, if not more through our actions as we are our words. Remember the adage, "it ain't what you say but the way that you say it"? This is exactly the case with presenting.

Neutral or starting position
One of the most important things, which can take a few attempts to master, is to develop a camera-ready resting position, and get used to being in neutral. A neutral position usually involves being square to the camera, facing it head-on. As noted, keeping an open, balanced, upright, stable stance is our presenting foundation, and standing square-on to the camera creates a connection with the audience. You'll be relaxed (without slouching) and your shoulders will be nice and open, not scrunched-up.

However, many people wonder what to do with their hands. You can let them hang at your sides, but you'll likely be fighting the urge to swing them, or fidget, and it can look a little odd. I normally advise people to have one hand resting in the other, however is comfortable, held around the waistline. Pro-tip: It's important not to hold your hands defensively in front of your groin, as if you're about to field a penalty shot in a soccer game! Covering the pelvis, or the so-called 'fig leaf' is a defensive position and makes us look nervous, not a good way to start an interaction. It also pulls the shoulders in and closes our bodies visually. We are open, we are vulnerable, and that makes the audience trust what we're saying much more. From neutral you can easily move your hands to make gestures.

The Three Gesture Sets

Gestures are extremely powerful visual cues, and we can employ them to great effect when we want to communicate ideas, scale, importance, or tone. When on camera, we're often told to be mindful of over gesticulating, as it can be distracting. Small movements look bigger on screen, and too much movement can quickly become wearying to the viewer. Therefore, how much you move, and how often, needs to be a conscious decision on camera. That said, the relative 'size' of your movements and gesticulations is also determined by how close the camera is on you (see Chapter 5). Some shots, like a 'mid' or 'wide' leave more space around the subject (you) and leave you a lot more room to play with.

Another consideration is that a study performed by Vanessa Van Edwards at the Science of People research centre, found that Ted Talk presenters who had the most hits and were voted most charismatic gesticulated almost twice as much as those who had lukewarm responses. This indicated a correlation between our gestures, and perceived charisma. However, it is worth bearing in mind that there's a big difference between on-stage presentations and on-screen presentations, where movements are more noticeable. Yes, Ted Talks are filmed, but never in close-up, and as mentioned, a wide shot is much more forgiving of movement. My advice here is this: be mindful of your gestures but don't be afraid to use them *when they add suitable emphasis* to your points. Gestures are also a powerful memory tool for both you and your audience. They can keep a point in mind, as well as drive it home. Consider a gesture *plan* as you rehearse your material, and make notes on your script, if you have one, to remind you where you might want to bring home a point with a gesture! Use your plan as a prompt for where you want to indicate significant points, numbers, strong emotions, that kind of thing.

Simply put, use gestures strategically, and wisely. Don't just flail your way through a presentation hoping that more arm movements equal more charisma, because I assure you that doing it wrong is worse than not doing it at all! Let's look at developing some good gestural habits for our nvc, or non-verbal communication. Here are three common gesture sets and contexts in which to use them.

No. 1 The 'give'

This is an open hand 'reading a book' pose – you can use this to give options and facts, without resorting to pointing. For instance, if you're using two different ideas or groups to note division, you can indicate with your right hand to denote one side, and your left hand the other. You then have the option to refer to each hand as a cipher for that concept, highlighting the appropriate hand when making a point. This works as a memory stimulator and reinforces your words with a gesture. You also have the option to separate or bring these categories together, by moving your hands closer or further apart should you want to reinforce notions of unity or separation.

No.2 The 'show'

This gesture has the greatest variety and tends to *message match*, i.e. is congruous with the topic and the feel of a piece – It can be used to measure numbers (holding up three fingers) "I'm going to cover three points", and magnitude (arms wide), "there was a huge response", vs (fingers pinching an imaginary cherry) "this is a very small minority". Growth or decline can also be indicated by making a signal like a plane taking off or descending with one hand, "there was a huge growth in sales" vs, "there was a decline in sales."

It's recommended that you always match the message when presenting numbers that indicate talking points, but not if you're relaying financial news, as obviously it's not appropriate or practical to highlight thousands and millions in stock markets this way.

The 'show' can also be used to convey emotion. When conveying emotional vulnerability or meaningful topics, it's most effective to gesture to the chest and heart region, as it stimulates the feelings we associate with that region. For example, "I want to talk about an issue that means a lot to me" (indicating heart region). As you can imagine, this gesture can also be used to indicate the mind (by pointing to your head), to make mental notes, which are very useful for denoting points worth remembering.

No.3 The point, or chop
This is perhaps more useful in business meetings than it is on screen, as both pointing and chopping at the camera (and thereby, the audience) are quite aggressive unfriendly gestures. Only use these sparingly, if all.

Other considerations
In general, having your palms facing up is generally regarded as more accessible than palms facing down. Keeping your hands in view, especially when open palms face the audience, tends to make you look more trustworthy. We instinctively trust somebody who appears to have nothing to hide. However, this can look strange and awkward, and we don't want to go through a presentation looking like a hostage at gunpoint, so only sprinkle in an open palm in a greeting or signoff. A simple wave or open armed welcome can do wonders to make your audience invest in you.

In Summary

Try not to let gestures become tiresome or wearying and try to remember not to wave and flail your arms through a presentation (there's a funny sketch about this by Mitchell and Webb). In addition, it doesn't look great when a presenter's arms 'cross' their body or close off the connection between presenter and audience, so avoid crossed arms or self-hugging postures. Avoid putting your hands on your hips or in your pockets and try to avoid letting gestures be an excuse for bad tics and habits, such as self-comforting and fidgeting.

Remember,

The Give – open hand 'reading book' pose (usually only employing one hand at a time) – gives options and facts

The Show – large variety – matches message. Congruency and creativity.

The Chop/Point – chopping pointing hands, strong opinion. One or both hands. Use sparingly if ever!

Use gestures to <u>underline</u> or em**bolden** your words. Imagine gestures are the Nonverbal equivalent of underlining a script or using a bold font. You wouldn't want it all over every page, but it certainly has its place when you can back it up with intonation and intent. Also use gestures as a memory tool – gestures are great placeholders in your dialogue and can be used to great effect to make your presentation memorable and impactful.

Gestures are a great way to engage more physically with the audience journey, and a good place to channel nervous energy, if used correctly. But use them as the seasoning of the meal not the main course, the colour of the tapestry, not the fabric, and you'll be on the right track!

Exercise 4. Observation of Posture

Get somebody to take a picture of you standing or sitting naturally, or if alone, stand in front of a mirror but turn off your mirror pose. Let yourself relax into your regular way of standing, or sitting as if you're just in the kitchen, making tea, not thinking about it too much.

Ok hold that pose and try to observe objectively – what do you see? I have a habit of letting my mid and lower back relax, which slumps me forward onto my stomach, and pushes the tummy out. Many people stand or sit like this, particularly when in an office chair.

Take note of your own habits and recreate them intentionally now. Observe how they feel in the body and make a mental note to try to catch this behaviour when it happens.

Remember, the three key points are; Observation; Inhibition; and Direction. Let's go through them again here for ease of reference.

1. Observation is a mindfulness of our posture. Try to be mindful of where the weight rests when you sit or stand, and how balanced you are on each side of the body, noting any slouching or poor posture.
2. Inhibition is holding back from bad habits, whilst being careful to only employ an *appropriate* level

of effort. i.e. not going too stiff and making things worse!
3. Direction is the process of sending specific instructions or thoughts to the body to encourage space and blood flow rather than contraction and tension. This is all managed by the relationship between the head, neck and spine.

Exercise 5. Gesture Plan

Think about a gesture plan for the following script. Imagine the context of this presentation (in front of a monument) and where gestures might be required. Write on the script where you might want to use a gesture, and which kind (Show, Give, Point), it might require.

Hello, I'm (your name).

The term, 'Cleopatra's Needle' is actually a misnomer. It's an Egyptian obelisk from the reign of Tuthmose III. This is what we call a cartouche and it holds one of the names of the king...
(indicates cartouche)
...in this case Men-Khefe-Ra. He reigned 1,000 years before any Cleopatra reigned in Egypt. It's also 3,000 years before it came to rest on London's embankment. The history of the needle is quite remarkable. It was originally one of a pair erected at the entrance to the Temple of the Sun in the ancient city of Heliopolis near Cairo. It stood there for over a thousand

years but was overturned during an invasion by the Persians in the fifth century BCE.

500 years later, it was resurrected, and placed outside a temple dedicated to Julius Caesar in Alexandria, where it stood for thirteen centuries! It toppled in a major earthquake but was once again excavated in the early 1800s. The needle became a gift presented to Great Britain in 1819 by the ruler of Egypt, Mohamed Ali.

Now give it a practice run. Film it if you want to, but for now just concentrate on putting all the elements together and getting your delivery nice and smooth.

5. Introduction to Camera

You may be an experienced presenter at conferences or meetings but presenting to camera involves a specific set of skills based around the way cameras capture your performance. Because presenting on camera involves a tightening and honing of your skills, it can translate into non-camera presenting quite well, but the other direction, coming from a stage or live presentation background to camera work, will require some honing.

First, I want to give you an overview of what being on camera means. Let's think about the camera for a second and how it perceives its subject, in this case, you, or me. What the camera captures and how much, is determined by framing. it's good to know a little about different types of shot, so that you'll know how much of you is being captured - that is to say, is in frame.

- A wide shot is just that. It captures as much of the scene or room as possible, including most likely any part of you that isn't obscured by a person or object in front of you.
- A medium shot will be a little closer in and may cut off your lower half. This is a common shot in shows with presenters and experts.
- A close-up is what most of us are used to seeing when 'talking heads' are present, such as on the news or history and science programs. The shoulders and head are in view and you still get a sense of the person's surroundings.

- Finally, a tight, 'very', or 'extreme' close-up focuses primarily on the face, ignoring body and background.

As an expert commentator or presenter (and even as a 'talking head'), you'll most commonly be shown in medium to close-up, with multiple shots jumping between the two when emphasis is needed. Next time you watch somebody on television, watch out for this. We're so used to it as viewers that we don't even notice that the jump is happening half the time. Close-ups and extreme close-ups create a sense of focus and intimacy between the subject and viewer, and this is important, because it determines how a person comes across on camera. This means that details such as your micro-expressions will be easily picked up on, so it's important to learn how to control these whilst also appearing confident, relaxed, sincere, and authoritative. Sounds like a lot of work! It's true that there is far more to presenting than meets the eye, and competent presenters just make it *look* easy...but don't be deterred. I'm going to take you through everything you need to know to get on camera and present with the best of them!

Expression

Setting your Camera Face

One thing I've noticed as a dead giveaway as to whether somebody has had camera training is this –

Imagine the camera rolls now

Presenter Deadpan

Presenter Smiles
'Hi – My name's Paul, and I'm here to teach you about presenting on camera!'
Presenter Deadpan
Cut

To clarify, if you're not smiling at the very start of recording, or after you finish speaking, you're creating a window of doubt for the viewer. The result is that it makes everything in between those two unfortunate resting faces seem ingenuine, i.e. it makes us look fake. This highlights the importance of setting your camera face, and it's one of the most *crucial things* to remember to do, even if everything else falls by the wayside. If we're not holding a positive, ready expression **as soon as that camera rolls**, our audience, who will judge us in the first 7 seconds, remember, turns off figuratively, and probably literally.

There's something called the *facial feedback hypothesis* which states that our expressions don't just reflect our emotions, but they actually influence them. Expressions are also contagious and transmit what we're feeling subconsciously to our viewers. Basically, we catch emotions by seeing them. Do you see where this is going?

If you start a presenting piece looking dour-faced you are setting yourself up for failure as soon as somebody sees that expression. They will subconsciously 'catch' that emotion and that will influence their opinion of you and your work without them even being able to put a finger on what it is that they don't like. Of course, this is also contextual, and we can't be grinning when delivering bad news, so it's important to get to know your face and master your expressions, so that you have a range of context-appropriate and empathic expressions to fall back on.

Micro Expressions

Micro-expressions are usually reactions over which we have no control, which flash across our faces too briefly to be noticed consciously. However, because the camera magnifies everything we do, micro-expressions become that much more noticeable, even subconsciously. Have you ever noticed how when you see an uncomfortable presenter it makes you also feel uncomfortable or maybe even embarrassed? It's important that we are transmitting the right emotions through our body language and expressions. Whilst micro expressions aren't something we can always control, by preparing for the camera with breathing, vocal and posture exercises, and prepping our camera face, we can minimise the effects of any negative emotions (particularly nerves) showing through.

Expression and Context

Whilst many generalist presenting guides might encourage you to slap on a smile, as an on-screen expert, there are of course contexts where this won't be appropriate. Perhaps you present serious financial news, or medical updates, and it's certainly never appropriate to be smiling when presenting tragedies or bad news. In the absence of a smile, sincerity and passion become paramount. Additionally, without a smile there to bolster brain endorphins, we need to be animated enough that the audience knows that you find the material interesting, as this prompts them to find it interesting too. But the level of animation should *match the message*, you don't want to be gesticulating too wildly, for instance, if the piece is meant to be understated. Equally, gestures, as we have covered, can be used to great effect to enhance your apparent excitement or level of interest regarding a subject, so even where it isn't appropriate to smile, you can still employ gestures to enhance your performance.

Just remember to message match – keep your performance at the level of the piece that you're presenting and employ these techniques to help you seem naturally enthusiastic about your subject!

Recording vs Live – what you need to know

Whilst shooting live can be nerve-wracking, it's quite rare that as an expert or thought-leader you'll be presenting live, unless it's in an interview setting.

Recording – the pros and cons

The big change in recent years is the revolutionary impact that digital technology has had on the field of filming. Digital recording and editing have taken what used to be the territory of professional filmmakers and put it into the hands of everyone. One of the main benefits for us as presenters, is this means digital recording is cheap! The practical result of that is that you can now do as many takes as you need, schedule notwithstanding, to get the results you want. On a set, this is invaluable, although it can mean unnecessary perfectionism. If you happen to get an inexperienced director, or you are recording for yourself, it can be all too tempting to do too many takes.

This has benefits and drawback. Yes, you may finally get a take without any technical mistakes, but you may find that after the first two takes, energy drops and the earlier takes seem better, despite minor mistakes. As such, it can be worth learning to live with a few small errors here and there (I know I've had to!). Often the sweet spot is those first few takes, where the excitement and energy are still fresh. After that you get diminishing returns but try not to put too much pressure on yourself. Remember, a relaxed presenter is better than a technically perfect, yet uptight presenter!

Going Live!

Live usually means that there's no delay between recording and transmission, though often networks will keep a delay, between a few seconds and a couple of minutes, for the sake of live editing and censorship.

Whilst recording live does mean that any mistakes cannot be corrected, there are also benefits to this type of work. Firstly, live performances have an energy and pace that recorded sessions don't and can be very enjoyable to be a part of. Secondly, you're never forced to endure multiple takes, and nobody expects absolute perfection. Even viewers at home realise that on live shows, 'anything can and does happen' so we've been conditioned as an audience to ignore minor slips and imperfections. That worst-case scenario that you dread is rarely more than a slight stumble which you will simply breeze past in a live show and move on to other things. The most important thing when working live is to KEEP GOING no matter what. Ignore mistakes, don't let them trip you up, and accept that you're fallible and human. If you can let the bad moments pass without letting them frustrate or exhaust you, you can learn to love working live for the high that it delivers.

Live interviews

As formal or informal conversations, these are the easier task in many ways, as you should naturally get drawn into the conversation and forget about the cameras. In interviews you will almost never look directly into the lens (unless you're the host introducing the show) and your interactions will be more natural than when you present to camera.

As an expert

The only times I've had to present 'live' as an expert were 'live' live in the loosest sense. They were recorded interviews that were only going to have minor edits, so as not to break the flow of the conversations. I've also had to record live for the news, and that was more daunting at first, but again, once you're there you get drawn into a conversation rather than having to ad lib into a camera lens. Simply put, it's generally much easier to appear in interview as an expert than if you must host a live show yourself.

Hopefully the above will alleviate some concerns, if any of you have any trepidation about recording in a studio or appearing in live interview. Remember, people make mistakes, we occasionally jumble words and we move on. We'll cover this in more detail, but for now know it's enough to just keep calm and carry on. Don't acknowledge mistakes, or if the context is right, just laugh them off and <u>keep going</u>.

In a recording context you can just go again from the top, or perhaps do a new take. It's best to ask in each specific circumstance what your director or d/o/p prefers. Just know that everyone makes mistakes when live and our brains very quickly write over them. If we don't panic or make a big deal out of mistakes they're quickly forgiven and forgotten. Just breathe, fall back on your training, and move forward!

Where to look on camera

So, you're about to get in front of the camera for the first time, but how do you address the camera, if at all? The answer depends on the context.

If you're doing a *piece to camera*, then you'll be looking straight into the lens. This is the most common form of self-filming, where you're directly addressing your audience. At first this can feel quite alien, because whilst we're used to looking at people on screen, talking into the dead eye of a lens without breaking eye contact can feel unnatural and unnerving.

There's a simple trick we can apply here to make dealing with the camera even easier. Imagine that the camera is a close friend or family member, ideally somebody you would feel comfortable saying anything to. You want to talk to the camera as if it's that person, one single person, and don't think about the number of people you're addressing.

This is important, because we speak differently to individuals than we do to a crowd, and we need to make each individual watching feel like we're addressing them, or risk we risk losing that person. I see several aspiring YouTube presenters breaking this rule, for example they'll be trying to think of what to say next, and maybe meandering around the topic, looking off to the left or right, or worse, looking down. You may notice how suddenly you as the viewer feel less engaged and the presenter seems less interested in the topic, the audience, and overall far less professional.

There are sometimes exceptions, but you'll notice that the more a presenter looks away from the lens, the less engaging they are and the less interested in you they appear to be. If you really struggle to talk into a lens there's an old trick from television studios that you can employ. Some presenters would bring a photo of a friend or loved-one and tape it to the casing of the camera (usually just below the lens). They would then talk to the photo as if addressing their friend, to help calm nerves and warm their performance. Again, it's vital to talk to your audience as if they're individuals, not just an amorphous lump, as this sets the level of intimacy needed to really engage through the camera. So, remember, eyes on the lens!

Some exceptions

When conducting interviews or being interviewed the host will usually look into the lens when they introduce the topic and guest, and from that point on the host looks only at the guest, unless they're making an aside specifically to the audience.

If you're a guest on an interview you will usually only look at the host and speak to them. This may seem obvious, but studios can be disorienting. I've been in situations where guests thought that they needed to address the camera when answering interview questions, but often the opposite rule applies – when being interviewed, never look into the lens …unless you're co-hosting!

Co-hosting

Things become a little more complicated when co-hosting, and this is an acquired skill for most. Co-hosting is like presenting in that when speaking to the audience, you need to look directly into the lens, but here's where the rules are relaxed a bit. If you reference your co-host or address them, you can look at them as you do so, and speak between yourselves to an extent. However, be careful not to do this for too long, or you'll once again lose audience engagement.

But what about when your co-host is speaking? Where do you look?

Well, you can look into the lens and at your co-host. You shouldn't linger too long on your co-host, for the reasons mentioned above, and you should appear engaged in what they're saying no matter where you're looking. The best way to achieve this is to actively *listen* to them. Listening is important when co-hosting and when conducting interviews, as we'll see when we cover that topic.

Another exception is when handling objects. Whilst this is most commonly associated with shopping channels, it's also highly relevant to science communicators, archaeologists, technology bloggers and anybody who performs 'unboxing' videos and the like.

In this instance, you will normally start by speaking to camera, but then you'll naturally look at the object when handling it or pointing out details. So, in this instance, feel free to look back and forth between object and camera, and just remember to keep up the engagement and not get too distracted in what you're handling (though focusing on details can be fascinating for targeted audiences, of course!).

Talking heads

Yet another exception is the 'guest expert' or 'talking head.' This is the typical setup you tend to see on documentaries or news programs, where a person, usually an expert of some kind, is seen talking to somebody 'off camera' as if answering a question or presenting details on a topic. Having done a number of these I can tell you that there isn't always somebody to address offside/behind the camera, as the camera person may be under their hood, and the director may be watching from the side-lines. Occasionally you'll be talking to a blank wall or point in space, instead of talking to the camera, so that they can film you talking, as if to somebody off camera.

Other times somebody may sit in opposite you, just off camera so you can address them instead. It varies with the production, but the result is the same. You may have a prompt device or script held up for you off camera, if you're lucky, but more often, you won't. The trick is to pretend that you're addressing a friend, as with talking into the lens.

Dealing with multiple cameras
The idea of dealing with multiple cameras may be scary, but the reality is that for most thought-leaders and experts it's simply no different than dealing with one. The reason for this is unless you are hosting a live studio television show (sometimes called a magazine format show) you'll only ever be addressing one camera anyway and often not even that. If you look at the format of most shows with 'talking heads', or experts, who sit talking about a specialist subject, you'll notice that they mainly speak off camera, to somebody who appears to be standing to the side.

When in a TV studio for instance, a show host will often have in-ear feedback telling them which camera they'll be speaking into next. The cameras may have lights to indicate which one is live, but again, that's not something you need to worry about as an expert presenter. In ten years of working both in front of and behind camera, I have never been asked, nor have I ever asked anyone, to present to multiple cameras in real-time.

If there are multiple cameras on you whilst you are being filmed, the additional cameras are usually just to get different angles to cut between in the final edit, and you don't have to worry about addressing or even acknowledging them. This is perhaps the clearest exception to the 'always speak into the lens' rule.

To summarise; the golden rule of presenting is to always look into the camera lens ... except when it isn't! But the key thing to remember is to engage your audience, and remember that one, friendly, individual that you're presenting to. If you present like you're addressing an individual, and not a mass, you can't step too far wrong.

Walking on Camera

There will be times that you'll be asked to walk and talk on camera. Whilst these are things that we're usually quite proficient at doing, it is striking how quickly coordination can disappear under pressure, so it's good to know a few tips and hacks to get this important skill under your belt. Take it from me, don't let an audition or actual recording be the first time you practise this skill, as it comes up more than you might expect. Usually, walking and talking involves no more than that - but entry and exit points can vary.

Entry

Sometimes you'll be asked to simply start from a certain point with the camera already on you. Top tip – take a couple of steps to get into the flow of your walk before you start talking so that your editor has some footage to cut into. Sometimes you'll be asked to walk into frame (that is, onto camera). When doing this make sure that your *expression is ready* and that your *eyeline meets the camera* when you step into frame. Don't start talking off-camera unless otherwise directed, as this can appear strange.

If you need to determine an entry point based on your script, or need to know how far you're to walk, start from your intended end-point, known as your 'mark.'

Now you're going to walk towards the start point, talking through your script at your intended pace until you reach the end of the script. Stop here. You've found your starting point based on the length of the script. This is where you'll start walking & talking. But remember to add a couple of extra paces in for safety and as warmup steps. Voila! You have found your start point!

Exit points

sometimes you'll be asked to simply stop in front of the camera. Remember not to stop talking just because you stop walking. Relax into position, anchor yourself in for your last few lines or words and finish what you have to say. Sometimes you'll be asked to exit frame after you finish speaking. This can be one continuous movement, that has you walk and talk as you move on and off camera. Alternatively, you might walk on, speak, then walk off. Just remember to have your camera face on and deliver that exit line with the same focus that you would if standing still. Unfortunately, your audience doesn't care that you're having to juggle your lines with where to walk next! Then exit camera as smoothly as you can, taking direction regarding where you should be looking as you do (usually it's the point that you're walking to, off camera). It sounds like a lot, but usually all falls into place after a couple of practice runs.

Hitting a mark

This is a skill shared by actors and presenters, but lucky for you we tend to have it easier. Hitting a mark tends to mean just reaching a certain point in front of camera, so wherever they say to hit on the ground, just try to find a visual reference point in your peripheral vision, or gauge the distance from camera, as you won't be able to physically look down at your mark when you're doing a take! Usually its best to gauge your distance and relationship to the camera when standing on the mark, and then try to walk back to that.

Other tips

Separate your walking and talking pace – just because you speed up or slow down your walking, doesn't mean you speaking pace should change, and vice-versa. The key is to find a pace for both, which are complimentary.

If your camera operator is walking with you, try to match their pace or use a nice steady pace that they can match. Trust me, they'll appreciate it!

Remember your posture when walking on camera – just because you can't anchor into place, it doesn't mean that posture goes out of the window. Remember, shoulders relaxed and down and back, natural good arch in the lower back, head over your body, not protruding forward. Imagine your top half 'gliding' and try to walk so that you don't bob up and down or sway excessively from side to side.

Lastly, the better you know your material, the more mental energy you must devote to your movements, so when you start out in presenting, try to learn your material as well as possible, and give yourself every chance to excel on screen!

Exercise 6. Putting it all Together Part 1

You're now ready to start pulling these various skill sets together. We're going to do another presenting exercise, like the first video you did, which we called 'control.' Like that video, this will be unscripted, and you're going to talk for around a minute stating your name, your pastime or occupation, your areas of special interest and what you think you can bring to camera which is exciting or new. Next, you're going to take the Self Evaluation sheet from the Appendix and watch your new video.

Mark your answers on a separate sheet of paper and try to be objective as possible.

What might a stranger think of this performance? If you're feeling very brave, ask a friend or colleague to assess you. Don't let negative feedback deter you. You're still new at this, and presenting is a life-skill that everyone (including me!) needs to continually develop and improve.

Don't worry about areas we haven't covered yet, you can fill those in later. Keep the Self-Evaluation sheet handy for your following videos. Note improvements and where you may be struggling. And don't worry, it will come with practice!

6. Writing Scripts

If you're presenting for your own channel, you'll likely be coming up with your own scripts and materials. This gives you the freedom to simply create a list of talking points and ad lib through your topic at your own pace!

However, when working for a production, sometimes you'll be asked to write a full script, or edit material given to you and adapt it into a script, and this is especially common for what we call 'talking head' appearances.

Often, you'll be given some research or information. I always advise fact-checking this research as production assistants assigned to these duties will almost never have the same expertise in your subject that you do. Either way, it's wise to get proficient at writing and editing scripts and doing so quickly.

Something I've struggled with as an academic, and something that you may also battle if you're from a background dealing with complex jargon, is writing in complex language. There's a tendency for academics to write long run-on sentences or go the other way and overcompensate with clipped language. The key here is to write the way you would normally talk and assume no prior knowledge if presenting to a general audience. Whilst it's perfectly acceptable to use legal jargon or complex financial terms for specialist shows and channels, you'll quickly lose your audience if you try to do that with the general public.

Even if you don't come from a field of complex jargon, we still tend to write in more complex ways than we speak. I spent years learning to write in academia, and I've spent just as many re-learning (and un-learning) those tools in order to write and fix scripts. The fact is, writing in a clear manner, that works for the mouth and ear, is very different to writing on paper. One way to quickly gauge whether your script is vocal-ready is to *read it aloud*. Notice how awkward some lines are, and how long certain sentences last. This is a key step to getting your script ready for camera and should never, ever be skipped! In addition, here are thirteen tips to help you craft the perfect presenting script: -

1. If you have a lot of ideas you need to get down, try hashing out a mind map or spider-gram. Now use this as a guide to verbalising what you want to say about the topic.
2. Using a phone or Dictaphone, record what you say. There are plenty of apps available to help you do this, which automatically turn your words into text. Send this to yourself and use it as a springboard for your script.
3. Try writing for the mouth, not the eye. What we hear is processed differently to what we read. Try conversational language over technical language.
4. Verbalise everything. Always read your scripts out loud and edit anything that sounds awkward.
5. Use shorter sentences than you would when writing for a reader. Holding too many sub-clauses in the mind makes it hard to keep track of emphasis. It can also ruin your flow on camera.

Run-on sentences are also harder to read on prompt machines.
6. Use pauses. If you write in pauses, you'll have a better idea of how to pace yourself. This also allows you to plan for your next breath, which helps stop you from getting hoarse.
7. Use <u>underline</u> or *italics* in the places in a script where you think you need to add verbal emphasis. Sometimes when presenting we disengage from what we're saying, particularly when reading from a prompt, so visual cues are useful.
8. People listen to shows as much as they watch them, so aural delivery is even more important since the advent of mobile phones and tablets.
9. Break your content down into a journey for the listener.
10. Avoid long lists of jargon and statistics. These will make people's brains switch off.
11. Write out numbers in word rather than symbol form. This helps you keep pace with a prompter if needed.
12. Make your opening and closing sentences as punchy as possible. Grab people's attention and be memorable.
13. Finally, write something you'd want to watch!

Editing Scripts.

The same principles apply to material that you're given. Check with your producer or director if you're expected or allowed to rewrite the script into your own words. Now apply the above to the material, making sure the structure works for you, and sentences are concise without being clipped. Often it doesn't take much work to get a script just how you like it and working on it can also help with memorisation and delivery!

Timing Scripts

The ideal pace for vocal delivery on camera is around <u>three words per second</u>. Knowing this means that you can write your scripts with a specific length in mind, which will help you write a piece that fits your schedule.

So, without even timing your read-through, you know that if you need a piece that's 1 minute long, that's sixty seconds. At three words per second, you'd need to write a piece roughly 180 words long, to fit that time frame. Of course, words have different lengths and some sentences need more careful diction, and as such, the three words per second rule, is more of *a guideline*. We still need to time our read throughs after we've written a piece to know how close we are to our ideal script length. One good thing is that this forces us to read our script out loud again, which will help iron out any stumbling points.

Memorising scripts

Whilst prompt technology is common these days, it's always wise to have a good understanding of the material that you're about to present, if possible. Even if a shoot intends to use a prompt, I've had experiences where the technology hasn't worked properly, or I've had to do a walking-talking piece where the prompt is too far away for me to see. Other times a director might want a less formal approach or may be looking for the natural energy that accompanies ad-libbing.

As such there will be times when you simply must know the material you want to talk about without a script, and that's when you have to get, what actors call, 'off-book.' This means that you've memorised enough of the material that you no longer need to refer to your pages. This is one of those times where, unfortunately, presenters have it tough. Actors may get days or weeks to memorise lines, and presenters often get less than a day. To make things worse, script changes are frequent, and you'll often need to memorise newer versions.

So how do you get off-book at a moment's notice? Well, the answer is the same as with most presenting skills; practice. But here are eight top tips to aid you on the road,

1. Break the script into multiple parts – segments are easier to memorise than pages, so break it down visually *and* thematically.
2. Plan a visual journey – if you're a visual thinker, you can associate different words or key concepts with different locations. Think of a route you know very well. Perhaps your house, or street, or journey to work. Associate key passages with stops or landmarks on that journey. This is how many

politicians memorise speeches. It's difficult at first, but with practice this can become second nature.
3. Master one section at a time – if you try to learn it all at once, even in segments, it may be overwhelming. Try memorising one bit at a time and mastering, at least the main points, before moving on.
4. Read it aloud – this is key in writing *and* in learning. Reading the script out loud will help reinforce your memory.
5. Count the talking points and use your fingers – remember when we covered gestures? Using your fingers to denote numbers is powerful for both the audience and in prompting your memory.
6. Understanding is key. A script you've memorised verbatim is no longer useful if there are last-minute edits. If you just memorised the words without *understanding* the content how can you ad lib, or adjust to the new script? Making efforts to engage with the script may seem painful, but it's key to both delivery and memory, so it's very important.
7. Try to pull out link words and concentrate on endings. If you remember how a piece ends clearly, it's often easier to remember how that section leads into the next. So, try to learn the links as well as the individual sections.
8. If you have time, leave gaps between learning sections, as this can help push it into your long-term, rather than short-term memory.

Sounds like an awful lot, doesn't it? Don't worry. The fact is, even on shoots where I've had pages of dense script to learn, you'll almost always be covering it one section at a time, so there's plenty of opportunity to break the script down into bite-sized, memorable chunks.

Remember, when you shoot in studios and with production companies, they don't expect you to be a memory master or some kind of machine. They only expect you to be courteous and professional and roll with any last-minute script changes. You'll need to check with your producer or director if the script needs to be learned verbatim (precisely word for word), or if you can improvise. Often, it's ok to re-order the script into something that better suits your own vocal delivery and style but there will be cases where this isn't possible for legal or branding reasons.

As such, always check before making your own changes, and get learning underway as soon as possible. This isn't academia, and the fact that you've memorised a script won't stop them changing it last minute. Just breathe deep, focus and you'll get the hang of it in no time.

Exercise 7. Talking to Time

Let's take another look at our sample script.

Hello, I'm (your name).

The term, 'Cleopatra's Needle' is actually a misnomer. It's an Egyptian obelisk from the reign of Tuthmose III. This is what we call a cartouche and it holds one of the names of the king...
(indicates cartouche)
...in this case Men-Khefe-Ra. He reigned 1,000 years before any Cleopatra reigned in Egypt. This was also 3,000 years before the needle came to rest on London's embankment. The history of the needle is quite remarkable. It was originally one of a pair erected at the entrance to the Temple of the Sun in the ancient city of Heliopolis near Cairo. It stood there for over a thousand years but was overturned during an invasion by the Persians in the fifth century BCE.

500 years later, it was resurrected, and placed outside a temple dedicated to Julius Caesar in Alexandria, where it stood for thirteen centuries! It toppled in a major earthquake but was once again excavated in the early 1800s. The needle became a gift presented to Great Britain in 1819 by the ruler of Egypt, Mohamed Ali.

Not including (your name), this script is 178 words long. At three words per second this is close to the ideal length for a one-minute piece (60 seconds x 3ps = 180 words). However, notice how the piece has some complex language, names and many numbers in it.

If you had one minute and twenty seconds to fill, what could you do to make this piece fit? Set a timer to go off in 80 seconds and record yourself talking to time. Is it pretty much on, or far faster? Don't stop presenting until the timer goes off. If you're on air and you run out of script you must learn to improvise by speaking more about the subject ("...which is why I find this so fascinating...") or including a link or passing over to a co-host ("Here's Tom with the weather!", "We're going back to the studio now"). Granted, as an expert your pieces will rarely require you to create links, but you will sometimes be required to talk to time, which means learning how you deliver a piece of a certain length - and how you can shorten and extend a script to fit the right window.

Now try delivering the same piece in 50 seconds. What can you do to make the piece fit? There's no single correct answer here, you just need to make sure you can learn to identify and prioritise the most significant information (in many cases you can just ask, or if speaking on your expertise, you'll know this intrinsically).

Objectively evaluate your performance using the included checklist!

7. Working with a Prompt

You're probably familiar with the prompt machine that broadcasters use to read us the daily news. Sometimes called a cue machine, or teleprompter, this was a machine developed by the company 'Autocue' in the late 1960s. Autocue is a brand name that became synonymous with the machine it produced around the world.

So, what is it for and how is it used? As we've covered, sometimes presenters need to deliver long stretches of text that they haven't had time to memorise, or which may be too much material to deliver accurately without reference. The prompter was developed for these instances. Initially it was a large bulky piece of equipment that you'd only ever find in a studio, but with the advent of touchscreen phones and teleprompt apps, you can use a prompt device almost anywhere now, including out on location, which would have been impossible even fifteen years ago!

The prompt works by having a screen with text rigged horizontally below an angled piece of reflective glass. The reflective glass is placed in front of the camera, and the text scrolls on the screen below. This text is reflected onto the glass, which the presenter then sees in front of the lens. The camera, however, doesn't pick up the text on the glass in front of the lens, just the presenter on the other side. This means the presenter can read their script off the prompt whilst appearing to look straight into the lens.

You can, with most prompt software, determine how large the font is, the sentence structure and spacing, and, most importantly, the prompt speed. In a traditional studio setting, an autocue operator would manually adjust the prompt playback speed to suit your delivery. You may remember from a previous lesson that the ideal talking delivery speed when presenting is around three words per second.

However, this doesn't mean by any measure that there is a standard prompt playback speed. Can anyone guess why? It's a mixture of things, from the structure of the script itself to the font size. The number of words displayed at any given time can vary greatly, and the more words there are to plough through on screen, the slower the prompt must go.

This works to your advantage, as it means that you can have a larger font if you're short sighted or if you need to stand further back from the camera. We'll cover this in more detail, but in general, the further back you stand when using a prompt, the easier it is to create the illusion that you're not reading. Why? Because the closer you are to camera, the easier it is to see your eyes moving over a script.

These days, especially if you're self-shooting, it's unusual to get a prompt operator on board. It's far more likely that you'll be using a form of prompt that uses a phone or pad device, which has a script loaded onto it, and a mobile rig. As such, you'll want to make sure the script loading onto it is up to date and doesn't contain any substantial gaps. Gaps will move with glacial slowness on screen and create awkward moments of 'dead air.'

It's possible, if self-shooting, to get some apps which only scroll when you speak, so it's worth shopping around and finding an app which works for you. It's worth the outlay, as presenting with a prompt, once mastered, is far easier than memorising lines and trying to improvise. Once you become proficient with this skill, it can be an absolute lifesaver, especially if you're working on projects with long scripts and last-minute alterations.

That said, it is a skill unto itself, with its own inherent pitfalls, so let's look at some techniques you'll need on camera when using a prompt.

Reading from a prompt

The teleprompter is a valuable device which can help you present huge amounts of text smoothly and accurately. That said, there's a science and art to using one. We've all seen presenters who are obviously reading to us, being very monotone and not engaging the text at all. Obviously, we don't want that, and it's important that the viewer can't tell that you're reading from a prompt. This can kill that sense of intimacy and rapport that we have worked so hard to cultivate.

Visual techniques - Line of sight

The first thing to know about using a prompt is where to look and how to interact with it. When you first start using a prompt, your instinct will be to read as you usually would from the top of the page, to the bottom. What happens if you do this on screen? Three things,

1. First your head (and chin) starts up high, and then drops as you read.

2. This then affects your eye line and makes it obvious that you're reading.
3. Worst of all, your head may move from side to side as you read across the lines.

Why is this a problem?

The lens behind the prompt screen is fixed, so only when you're in the middle of the 'page', will you even vaguely look like you're looking at the viewer. As we discussed at the outset, presenters should be looking straight into the lens to create a connection with the audience. If you start reading, and it's obvious that your eyes are moving away from the lens, you instantly break that connection. Luckily there are several visual tricks to create the illusion of not reading.

<u>This is key: you are letting the words follow you! You are never following the words.</u>

On a traditional Autocue device, there is a pointer roughly halfway up the screen, to indicate where your eyes should be resting and reading. Try not to move your eyes up and down the screen. You're reading the words on *that line only* and letting the autocue provide the next sentence for you on that line. That's what it's there for! I repeat, don't follow the words down the screen or try to race the prompt. If you're having to move down the screen to deliver the material at your set pace, one of two things are happening – you're either reading too fast, or your prompt is set to scroll too slowly!

A very minor adjustment to speed can make a huge difference. Your ideal line of sight is on that midpoint in front of the lens. Experienced prompt readers can look straight into that lens and read from their peripheral vision, which results in very little head or eye movement. You can see this on experienced news presenters, who appear to be talking to us directly, without using a prompt at all. This is rarely the case, as they only get the scripts just before they go on camera and rely on the prompt to a great extent. Try watching some expert news readers to see how they deal with the prompt device. You'll develop a new respect for how easy they make this skill appear! Of course, it helps a great deal if you already know the outline of your scripts, as the prompt is then only being used as a memory aid. A balance of learning and reading gives great results if you have time to study the scripts before a take.

Reading without Reading

Just as you shouldn't move your eyes around too much as you read a prompt, you also don't want to *sound* like you're reading to the audience. How do we accomplish this? If you haven't seen the script a certain amount of improvisational skill is needed here, so it really helps if you can get hold of the script beforehand. When I have a script to present that I know is going on a prompt device, I'll use italics and underlines if I need to emphasise certain parts of the script. Used sparingly, this is a very easy way to ensure you don't fall into monotone repetition.

The surest way to read without sounding like you're reading is to read in the same conversational tone that you'd speak in. This sounds obvious, but it can take practice in some cases.

The 5 key points are these,

1. Warm-up up your body and voice, as covered in other sections.
2. Check that there are not too many run-on sentences. As with script writing, long sentences with too many clauses are difficult to get right when improvising from a prompt. Use shorter sentences to avoid this problem. A rough guideline is if there are more than two commas in a sentence it may be too long for use on a prompt.
3. If you have time, practise a read-through of the script, noting any potential tongue twisters or stumbling points. Rewrite these as necessary, if you can.
4. Be mindful of pitch and tone – avoid monotone delivery, and add pitch, tone and emphasis as necessary.
5. Be mindful of your breathing. You can see where a sentence starts and ends on a prompt, meaning that you can this as a guide as to when to take your next breath. Remember what happens to the throat and voice when we strain due to lack of air? It gets dry and tired more quickly, so watch your breathing and stay hydrated.

Reading to Time
Also, remember these 6 general tips;

1. Don't race the autocue, let it follow you.

2. Keep your eyes on the mid-point of the screen where the lens is.
3. Avoid moving your eyes up and down or from side to side, as this breaks the illusion of intimacy.
4. Use the three word per second guideline, to keep your delivery at a smooth even pace.
5. If you stumble, keep calm and carry on! Pre-arrange with your director or DOP if they'd rather you start from the top of the paragraph or sentence if you stumble on a word. We'll cover this more later.
6. And, finally, relax! The prompt is here to help and serve you, not vice-versa! Go at your own pace, make the prompt match your speed, and use it as a tool to give the best performance you can without having to worry about remembering the details of a script!

Overall, I'd recommend using a prompt to everyone who wants to present scripted material. They are more affordable than ever, and with the advent of apps, almost anybody can use a phone or tablet and even build their own prompt device to help them present longer scripts.

It's so advantageous to be able to focus *on how* you're going to present rather than simply what you need to remember to present, and as such, I feel that a prompt machine isn't just a luxury anymore, but a vital tool in the arsenal of any presenter.

Exercise 8. Teleprompter practice.

If you don't own a teleprompter, don't worry. You're in the majority there! Whilst it's now possible to find both affordable and DIY teleprompters, you don't need one for this exercise. There are a few ways to do this exercise so do whichever suits you best. You only need paper and, preferably, a printer. You can also use a tablet pc screen, with any number of free prompt software apps, in addition to many free browser-based desktop prompt apps and websites.

The key components are that you are presenting from a script and recording your performance. You don't need to be looking straight into a lens for this, you just need the camera to pick up your expressions and delivery. As you're going to be practising presenting from a script, your eyes will always be on the script.

I advise that you find a sample script online for this exercise, as you'll likely want to print It out or copy and paste. The BBC has some free resources for news scripts, which you can cherry pick from. I'd suggest only using roughly a minute's worth of script, which you will now know is approximately 180 words. You can print these pages at a text size that you can see from several feet away, depending on your home setup. If you intend to stick the pages to a stand or wall and mimic the line of sight of presenting to camera, you'll need it to be at least 30-36 pt., depending on your eyesight. Alternatively cut and paste the script into prompt software on a desktop or mobile app.

Record yourself delivering the script. Note any stumbling points and revise these to better suit your diction.

Take note of the following:
- Did you stumble on certain words?
- How was your delivery speed compared to your control video?
- What prompt speed did you find most comfortable?
- Do you think you'd benefit from putting in more spaces between lines or paragraphs?
- How did you handle your breathing? Were you strategic, or did you just muddle through?
- How could you improve your breathing strategy and where could you build in pauses for breath in the script?
- How was tone and intonation? Were you monotone or did you sound convincingly conversational?
- How was use of gesture? How would you make a gesture plan for this and other scripts?
- Finally, how was your posture throughout? How did this help or hinder the other factors above?

8. Interviews

Even though they may seem to incorporate much of the same skill set, there is a huge difference between preparing to host an interview, and preparing to be interviewed, yourself. This is partly due to the differences in your ultimate goals for the interview. An interviewer wants you to reveal new, valuable, or exclusive information. They likely want a scoop. Whereas, when you're in the hot-seat it's your job to navigate the minefield of live questions and staying on message. Since being interviewed is more common for experts, let's start by looking at techniques to keep you comfortable, on track and out of the weeds. I'll follow this with some techniques and tips which have helped me a great deal when hosting interviews over the years, both on camera and in podcasting.

Being Interviewed

The first thing to figure out is if your interview is 'live to tape' or 'live broadcast.' If it's to tape you may get the opportunity to request a do-over on questions that go badly, or if the interview goes way off track. However, there's no guarantee that such a request would be honoured, so the best defence against this is to avoid falling into any potholes in the first place. This is especially important if your interview is live to air, so my advice is to treat every interview as if it's going out live and prepare accordingly.

Staying on Message

Know your message points by heart and memorise a list of things you want to cover. Count them off as you go, so that if the opportunity to add anything at the end comes up, you'll know if there's something you haven't covered.

Try to anticipate questions and prepare answers ahead of time. You can request questions, but often you'll only be told what rough areas you will be asked to cover, so work from the most likely avenues of enquiry. Base any prepared answers on such a list. You don't need to know it verbatim, but it will help avoid any curveballs.

Define your key message – irrespective of the questions themselves, you probably have a point you want to get across or even something you may want to promote, be it a service, a book, or tour, or cause. This isn't open license to bulldoze the interviewer, and you need to do this quite subtly so as not to appear antagonistic but try to steer the conversation naturally back to your key message by linking in to the questions you're being asked. You can say, 'this is what motivated me to do x' or 'I became interested in y because of this other thing…' practice, test it on peers, get feedback.

Keep your answers short, but not clipped. Don't just answer in the positive and negative – interviewers want you to expand on the topic. But don't give away too much. This is, again, a delicate line, that only you can decide for yourself. Some prefer to avoid long-winded stories and complex details, but equally, an emphasis on narrative and storytelling is becoming prevalent in interviews. Find the line you're comfortable with.

Keep in mind the length of the average sound-byte – this is approximately 7 seconds. These will often be 'pulled out' in promotional material, so make sure you prep potential sound bites to improve the odds that they'll use yours rather than pick out their own. Usually the most original or striking (sometimes controversial) material is picked – you don't get to choose here, so try to control your own narrative by having a few potential soundbites prepared to sprinkle into your answers.

Hold some material back - don't give everything away – especially if it's a new product or talk, or something you want people to buy. Keep them wanting more by giving tasters and teasers. Think of this as great potential promotional material for you and your work.

Tailor your approach and be an active participant in the interview. Involve the interviewer where you can. Depending on the context, it may or may not be appropriate to play verbal tennis or banter. For example, corporate or financial interviews focus less on personality and more on facts. On a show like Oprah, you'd get to be yourself, on Bloomberg, perhaps not so much.

Where to Look

Focus on the interviewer not the camera. Try to avoid looking around too much, even if you feel uncomfortable. Maintain a steady gaze on your interviewer, but not in an antagonistic or inappropriate way. Just keep a healthy amount of eye contact and be aware of when you look away. It's ok to look away, and look up when you're accessing your memory, as this is normal. Just avoid looking into camera unless directed to, and avoid shifting darting eyes, as this indicates untruthfulness.

In the Hot Seat

Try not to fidget and squirm in your seat too much. Try using the 'anchor-in' process discussed in the posture chapter, and apply those rules here – keep good posture, don't slouch, avoid swaying, avoid swivel chairs if possible, as they make temptation to move too high, avoid jogging knees and keep awareness of your body and movements as discussed previously. Gesticulation is ok, as gestures make us appear engaging and charismatic, but remain aware of your space, and the framing of the shot (See Chapter 4).

Use the breathing exercises included to relax and anchor into your space. Take a few deep breaths before cameras roll, if possible. Settle in and get comfortable without slouching. Use movement to your advantage. For instance, leaning forward emphasises a point and indicates interest and engagement. Whereas, leaning too far back can be inferred as disinterest or arrogance, so be mindful of that.

Watch out for so-called *filibuster* interviews. This is when interviewers aren't getting what they want, so they fill the time with excessive questions and reflection. This isn't always intentional, and as part of a two-way exchange it can take the heat off you a little bit. But when done aggressively, it's meant to hedge you out and stop you getting a point across, so if you're starting to feel side-lined by your interviewer, it is usually ok to cut in and make a point. You are there to speak and not just listen after all.

And finally, practice! If you know what questions or at least, what topics are coming your way, get a friend or colleague to run a mock interview with you. You'll be surprised at how easy it is to stray into the weeds, or off-topic, and at how much personal information you may end up revealing. Do a practice run if you can, whilst you hone your skills. Record it if possible, and listen back, noting any "umms" or "ahhhs." Make a mental note to avoid doing this, and pull yourself up, gently, when you find yourself doing this on camera. Whilst I *never* recommend acknowledging mistakes or stopping whilst recording, it's always good to stay mindful.

Conducting Interviews

There are several factors to a successful interview, and many of these rest in the hands of the interviewer. Conducting an interview isn't as simple as just asking a list of questions and trying to look good on camera. It involves genuine participation, understanding of the interviewee and their work, and insight – being able to pick out the most interesting nuggets that may be buried in responses.

The first rule of interviewing must be research. Knowing your subject gives you a huge advantage both on and off screen. When you first introduce yourself to your interviewee, they'll be impressed if you've done your homework, and perhaps equally insulted if you haven't. Naturally, you shouldn't overwhelm them with facts and figures about themselves, as that can overwhelming, but commenting on something you found interesting or asking about one of their own passion projects and interests shows that you care enough to put the work in.

Questions, Questions…

When you're working up a list of questions, or reviewing one researched for you, keep in mind that you may not get through all of them. It's smart to prioritise the questions that you want to ask, and to know which questions may lead naturally into areas you want to cover. Have a few big themes that you can tie disparate answers into if needs be.

It's also good to learn your questions, so that if the interviewee starts heading to that area, you have a natural link in. Equally, you should be careful not to ask closed, 'yes or no' type questions, as you'll find that some interviewees will be naturally less chatty than others. This becomes part of your research; finding out what your subject is like in interview, if possible. This will make life much easier for you if you know what to prepare for. If you struggle concentrating on interviewing and remembering what you need to ask, you can always keep question on you, or tape them behind the interviewee or on the floor. Don't put them next to the camera unless it's a remote interview however, as this would break immersion and eye contact.

The wording of the questions isn't all there is to consider. You should figure out what the ultimate aim of that question is, what key takeaways you want covered by that question, so that you can adapt on the fly if you need to. Don't just ask about their new project, ask them specifically about the process, or get them to describe an aspect of it that you know your viewers will find fascinating.

Keep questions open but be prepared to improvise. Go into new territory if you can. For personality-based interviews, ask them about their influences, their passions. Ask what makes them tick, ask what makes them unique or different, if anything? For more fact-based interviews, ask how this information may change preconceived ideas, why should we care, what does this mean for the future? Always remember your viewer, what they would find interesting, what they can get out of this.

Use deeper questions when you want to encourage your guest to speak in narrative. Stories naturally resonate with audiences and are more interesting than opinions and facts. Ask them how a process or key conversation went. Get them to describe as much as is natural.

It's incredibly important to listen to your guest, not just let them talk. Engage with what they are saying and pull out what you think is relevant and important. If they go off-track, try and pull them back in or have them focus on specific areas. It's your job to both enable your guest and to curtail them if they go into the weeds or spend too much time promoting their latest book or venture.

And finally, prepare more questions than you think you might need. If you have a time-frame to fill, you'll have to guess how much time an interview will take. Remember, cutting down is always easier than filling out. You won't get a chance to rehearse an interview (and to do so would harm the final product anyway), so think through the questions, the possible answers and try to gauge your guest's response time. If you know they speak in floral rambling language, you know you'll have to engage more to get what you're looking for and allow the time to do so. People who are shy or not forthcoming on camera may need more prompting and perhaps more segues into conversation, so more questions will be needed for the same time-frame. Equally, some nervous guests may ramble, and it will be your job to prepare follow-ups, pick out the best points, and get them back on track. You need to be careful not to stack your questions in this instance, however. Stacking questions is where you leave too little time between questions for the guest to answer properly. If done too often, it can seem aggressive and disrespectful, and will make your guest feel uncomfortable. It comes back to knowing your guest's work, what they're like in interview, if possible, and as much about them as you can learn that is relevant.

Your Guest

There's no one-size-fits-all approach to guests, as each will be unique and have specific needs, strengths, and flaws. As such, it's important to do everything you can at your end to prepare your interviewee. See how they feel about the process, reassure them, and talk them through the technical aspects of your interview.

Guests who are nervous on camera may benefit from some brief breathing exercises and the 'anchor in' process described in this book. Judge this on a case by case basis, and feel free to volunteer some tips to help them. A little can go a long way. You may also need to direct them where to look, or simply tell them to ignore the cameras and focus on the conversation as this tends to get good results. If you can lead a nervous guest into an area, they are knowledgeable or passionate about, they will naturally relax into the conversation, so try to keep that flow going.

It's a good idea to let your guest know in advance what areas you want to cover, but not a list of specifics. It's usually not a good idea to send specific questions ahead of time, but it is wise to ask them or their managers what topics, if any, may be off limits. This only applies in certain kinds of interviews, however. News pieces may be more interrogative and your job there is to steer somebody towards talking about subject they may not want to address. However, most subject experts and thought leaders aren't there to be interrogated, and you should be mindful of what kind of dynamic the interview requires, be it supportive and encouraging, or adversarial.

In specialist areas you'll rarely encounter a 'hostile witness', but you may be dealing with people who aren't used to being interviewed. If they're nervous it's your job to make them feel comfortable by creating a supportive and collaborative environment. Assure them that you're not there to catch them off-guard (unless you are, but you may want to rethink this strategy if you want future guests), and make your guests feel conversational by starting the process off-camera if possible. As you settle in to your seats you can reveal a piece of personal information or a vulnerability of your own. This often helps people feel more comfortable and sets up a good dynamic interplay once the camera rolls.

Leading from this, try not to interrupt the process with technical problems. Make sure cameras and mics are all set, and that your guest's microphone is properly positioned (particularly with lavaliere mics), because these small mistakes can render footage completely unusable. Prepare your environment as much as you prepare yourself and your questions. Always have a plan b (and c) if something breaks. As the saying goes, "two is one and one is none!" Provide water and refreshments if you're not in a studio, and be prepared for any special requirements.

As you can see, there's a lot more to interviewing skills than it may at first appear, but with preparation and diligence you can smash out a world-class interview even at the start of your career!

Exercise 9. Practice Interview

Ask a friend or colleague if they're willing to participate in a practice interview with you. Do your homework and write a few questions you'd like to ask. If they're unable to write questions to ask you, use the same set, and just keep them generic. Now set up a phone or camera to record you and take a turn each to both interview and being interviewed. Introduce your guest to camera when it's you're your turn to host the interview. Remember to address each-other, not the camera. Keep the lessons in mind and watch your interviews back.

- Did you stay on topic?
- As guests, did you manage to pepper your interview with your planned key points?
- What highlights or takeaways do you think would be used from this? Are they the same ones you would have intended?
- Evaluate your performance, noting the differences between talking to camera and talking to another person.
- Does it feel more natural?
- Did you find it easier?

Reflect on both the experience and recording and try to discern what you can bring away from the practice run when you go back to presenting into the lens.

9. Practical Presenting

Working as a presenter is a stimulating, highly rewarding career, and even if you never smash through into mega-stardom, you can still have many unique and exciting adventures working in front of the camera. But it's also a very challenging path, with many pitfalls. In this chapter we'll cover some of the day-to-day realities and difficulties of working as a presenter, in addition to a few lessons and techniques I've picked up over the years to help avoid the most common problems.

I've found that an understanding of the production process has been invaluable in helping me form a well-rounded understanding of my role as a presenter. It also stops me from jumping to incorrect conclusions when productions suddenly change plans or get shelved or cancelled. It's important to remember that ours is but a tiny (albeit important) role in the grander scheme of film making, and productions rarely revolve around a presenter. If a show doesn't cast you, you can't afford to take it personally. Equally, even when you are cast, there's no guarantee that a network won't change its plans, or that the show you signed up for will be the show that gets made. The stars align very infrequently to capture lightning in a bottle, and it pays to be realistic and pragmatic to avoid disappointment.

Working in 'Expert' TV

What's it like to work in television? As I'm sure you've already guessed, there are as many answers to that as there are performers, but there are some commonalities.

Generally, if you work on set and do any 'talking head' appearances, you'll have a producer, a director, sometimes a 'dop,' that's director of photography, a gaffer and spark, that's electric and lights, sound, and usually a host of production assistants or 'runners.' Is there a hierarchy? Yes, and the top of that totem pole isn't you, it's the producers and the director (and above them the execs and network). I'm telling you this because there's a danger of developing a sense of self-importance when you're treated like set royalty all the time. Trust me on this, presenters aren't expendable. In fact, when you're starting out, you're usually the most replaceable member of that crew.

You've likely heard the old maxim, 'be good to everyone on the way up, because you'll meet them all again on the way down.' Well, I'm sure that's often true, but I won't lie, you can meet some difficult people working in TV.

My best advice is this – try to stay humble and grateful. Stay on top of your skills and expert area. Never take any job for granted, and treat everyone you meet, especially the runners, with respect, because believe me, those runners will be producers before too long – as an anecdote, the runner from the first show I ever shot a pilot for is now a fully-fledged Hollywood producer. In eight years, his career trajectory shot him to the top, whereas I'm simply a more experienced version of what I already was. I'm not saying that presenting experience counts for nothing, but this is a cold hard reality check for aspiring presenters out there. So, be good to your crew!

Being an expert presenter isn't that unique a position to be in, even if you make the transition into full-time broadcasting. Many presenters are told to *develop an expertise*, in order to get more niche work. Whilst they may not have your depth of knowledge or experience, to a network or casting agent, you may be put in the same category. What does this mean in real terms? Simply that there's a lot of competition, even for jobs where you may be the foremost expert in the world on your topic.

So, expertise isn't a guarantor of employment. But it is an edge, and one worth keeping sharp. In my field, history and archaeology, I'm often approached about 'original research' – that is to say, production companies want to know what you're working on in your field already that they can jump in on. This saves them time and money when looking to break into new areas. Cheeky? Maybe, but that's the reality of this incredibly competitive field.

Casting

The casting process itself can be exhaustive. Sometimes you'll apply for a show and you won't hear back for months, if ever. That's not uncommon even if you're selected for a show, as network plans can change on a dime. It's not uncommon to get mixed or unreliable information out of production companies and networks, and as you can see, this isn't always their fault, or even intentional. It's a very changeable business.

I've been involved in castings that went through several stages and iterations, different contacts in companies, and even different networks. This process, understandably, takes time, so try to be patient and don't assume that no news means the project is dead. It can sometimes take a year or more to get the ball rolling on a new show. Bottom-line don't take anything personally. The same applies to casting. Actors out there know this well – if you *don't* get a job that you may think you're perfect for, it's not usually a reflection on your appeal or talents, but rather, producers tend to have a fixed idea of what they're looking for. Just like in an interview, the casting decision is usually made within the first seven seconds of meeting you, so if you're not right for a part, don't sweat it. Something more suited to you will come along, sometime with the same casting agent or producer. Remember to play the long-game, always be courteous, and with perseverance and diligence you'll get where you mean to go. But also remember that you need to protect your specialist reputation. Don't jump at every opportunity and be clear about what kind of projects you don't want your name associated with. For instance, I was once invited on a popular show about 'Aliens' and had to turn it down, despite what it might have done for my profile. Sometimes there is such a thing as bad press. In the long-run these decisions shape your career, so make sure you take castings that reflect where you want to be and how you want to be perceived in your field.

Auditions

It would be remiss to not touch on auditions, even though the process is somewhat different for subject communicators and experts. Unlike actors and many full-time presenters, you won't often be trudging along to open auditions for shows. It's more common in this field to be contacted, either directly, or through an agent (see below) and then asked to audition for a piece, frequently remotely. Remote auditions are becoming more common with the advent of Skype and similar programs, and they save production companies a small fortune in room hire and staff time. Where once a series of audition could take days in a studio, now a producer can get a feel if you're right for a project within minutes of a Skype call.

A remote audition often comprises you talking to camera (nearly always your own webcam) about yourself, your interests and background and whatever material the show being pitched will cover. The key thing here is that producers want you for your speciality, and you will usually be covering material with which you're at least passingly familiar, although there will be exceptions. The best way to prepare for auditions such as these is to practice. Self-record and practice introducing yourself, from your official title to where you studied or what institutions or organisations you represent. Research their topic and a little about the production company, so you know what kind of talent and tone they're looking for.

You'll want to dress appropriately for your field, and sometimes be asked to wear something specific (as an archaeologist I have been asked to wear an 'explorer-style' hat!). Avoid whites, as these throw off white-balance, and anything striped or overly patterned. Treat the audition as a test-run for whatever the show covers and adjust accordingly, just remember it's better not to go too over the top.

    The best advice I ever received regarding auditions was simply 'be yourself.' I refer you to the anecdote in the introduction to this book, and my not-so- auspicious screen debut (dressed as Indiana Jones and tied to a chair, no less). I mentioned the troubles I'd been having making the tape to my friend, an actress, who told me I was over-thinking it. I needed to roll out of bed, turn on record and talk, passionately, and authentically. Of course, I prepared the night before, readying the story I wanted to tell and making notes for myself in case I got stuck, but that next morning I followed her advice to the letter. I rolled out of bed (I didn't even brush my hair), turned on my camera phone, and started talking. I sent it in, forgot about it, figuring it would never pan out, and went on with my day. And you know what? Two weeks later I was in Hollywood shooting a pilot for a major network and having the time of my life.

Agents

    Actors and mainstream presenters often have agents, who help them find work and navigate contracts. Although it's less common to start your presenting career in the expert/communicator sector with an agent, it's not unheard of, and it's becoming more common. Agents fulfil a crucial role as mediator between producers, networks, and talent. There are many advantages to having an agent, as they can act as a key negotiator on your behalf, introduce you to an extended network of potential employers, and play the bad guys on your behalf in difficult negotiations, leaving your relationships with the producers relatively clear of friction. In addition, there are relatively few downsides to signing with an agent or agency, assuming it's the right fit for you both. It pays to find an agent or agency that suits your specific needs, and this can be easier said than done. For instance, if you're a top physicist and science communicator, it might be an obvious choice to contact Professor Brian Cox's agents, and see if they'll take you on their books, since they deal with those kinds of shows. This approach works for some agencies, who frequently deal with networks and producers creating that kind of content. However, some agents and agencies don't want to overlap their talent. They might hire a physicist, an historian and a botanist, but may avoid having two of each. The reason for this is often that they don't want to create a conflict of interest between their presenters. If two clients from the same company are interested in the same role, one of these clients will lose out either way (the uptick being, the agency still secures the job, though this is small consolation for the losing talent). There's also uniqueness to consider. Agents want to promote their talent as unique in their field, 'special,' as it were, and that's harder to do if you have physicists or botanists coming out of your ears! As with every rule there are exceptions. I was in the presenting stable of a company called Past Preservers for years. They have dozens of expert presenters from history and archaeology, and hundreds of similar experts in their database. The strength of the network and depth of resources makes up for any potential conflicts of interest for them. Presenters are often picked en masse, or as 'teams' for shows – allowing the agency and network to do better deals and giving presenters who might not have otherwise had a shot at that show a chance. It's a delicate balance and you must decide for yourself what cost/benefit ratio suits you, if any.

It's not always necessary to have an agent, particularly if you only work with networks occasionally, or oversee your own output exclusively. Then having an agent take commission (usually around 12-15%) can seem a frivolous expenditure. But when you're new to network negotiations, an agent will likely smooth the process considerably, in addition to making you their fees back and sometimes more. It's also worth bearing in mind that 15% on a deal that doesn't get sealed because you didn't know how to negotiate, is still 15% of nothing. As with all things, weigh up the pros and cons for your specific situation, but if you plan on a career in television, I'd advise at least considering trying to find an agent, and perhaps working with them on a trial basis to see if it's a good fit.

Finding an Agent

As with casting, the best way to find a suitable agent is often to find a list of possibilities and reach out with some good quality footage of yourself. Sometimes good quality self-shot video of you introducing yourself will suffice, but it doesn't hurt to have a showreel or link to some work you've done. Don't be disheartened if you don't get an agent straight away. Agents often don't want to take a chance with untested talent unless you can really prove you have that x-factor. But whilst this may run contrary to the above advice, it's worth noting that there is always a place for somebody with the right skill set, presence, and personality on camera. If you're in an industry that enjoys media attention, and you can master the exercises in these pages, you have a shot, and that's sometimes all you need.

But what are Agents looking for? Most often they want somebody who appears natural and can deliver on camera with confidence and enthusiasm. If you can convey your passion (we'll cover this below), and master speaking into the lens with fluency and coherence, then you're already head and shoulders above the competition. The skills and attributes most often cited as desirable are; an ability to talk about your subject with minimum fluffs and trips; experience or skill delivering short segments of rehearsed script; interesting look or personality; and, essentially, confidence!

Understanding how prompts and cue machines work will be a plus, as will the posture, breathing and warm-ups in this book, and familiarity with these professional techniques can be a valuable edge.

However, above all else, a positive attitude, respect for your peers and co-workers, and willingness to learn will take you far. Remember, the tv industry is relatively small, and your reputation travels faster and wider than any audition tape. Recommendation is invaluable to your ability to procure work, so build it wisely! As an addition to the above advice, when dealing with your agent, remember, they are often your closest ally when navigating the shark-infested waters of show business. You agent is also only privy to what they're being told by producers and execs, so don't hold them too accountable for information provided by third parties.

The Secret Ingredient

There's a secret ingredient to both human interaction and presenting of all kinds...

Passion. More specifically, energy and passion. We spoke about harnessing our nervous energy on screen and channelling it into excitement. This is great at first, when you have just the right cocktail of nerves and excitement, you can give powerful performances. But what happens as the nerves wear off? What happens when presenting becomes routine, or you're not enthused about your subject matter?

We spend most of our early careers learning how to relax on camera. We spend much of our later years (at least in my experience) being asked to turn up the energy. This is particularly true of American based castings, which emphasize enthusiasm and wonder. So how do you turn it on?

This is where that peppering of performance comes in, and we need to learn how to appear enthused and passionate without seeming fake or cheesy. The easiest way to do this is to try and work up as much genuine enthusiasm for your subject as possible. If all else fails, of course, you can rely on body language, expression, and intonation. The funny thing is that, because our bodies dictate mood as much as our brains in many cases, when you start smiling and acting energetically about a topic, you'll likely start to feel that way too.

It's vital to avoid a monotone or disinterested reading of the material. When you're on camera, YOU are the only one bringing energy to the piece, and you must deliver if you want to keep peoples' attention.

Sometimes, if you have a full crew, you'll get lots of encouraging feedback on set, and that's great. But if you're self-shooting, or working with a skeleton crew, you'll be the only one bringing energy to the space, and sometimes that can feel weird or over the top. If in doubt, ask. Or watch a take back if on your own. Different people are naturally more or less reserved or effusive. Find your 'normal' and practice turning up the energy as high as possible. Then bring it back in to a level that doesn't seem overwhelming. After a while, you'll find your own happy medium, and when working for others, they'll direct you based on the tone required for the show.

Try not to feel too self-conscious. Performance requires a certain lack of embarrassment, and faith in the final product. It's a fine line between *energy and passion* and *wild gesticulation*, so if you find yourself getting carried away, reign it back in. On a scale of one to ten, with one being dull and monotone and ten being screaming wild, aim for somewhere between four and six depending on the context. As an expert, you're expected to be knowledgeable and passionate about your subject. As a subject communicator or thought-leader, it's your job to convey that passion and get other people excited about it. So, don't be afraid to be excited about what you're presenting, as that can be contagious, and you should be contagious, too!

Tics and Habits

When I started on camera, I had so many bad habits, I thought I'd never be able to shake them all. But presenting is a life skill that we should keep developing our whole lives. Whilst we may never truly perfect it, consistent improvement is the name of the game, and the surest way to knock habits on the head is to watch ourselves back.

Common manifestations of nervous energy are fidgeting, restless limbs, jogging knees and facial tics. I used to lean my head too far to one side when presenting without a prompt because I was trying to access my memory on the fly. Things we do in our regular lives can look bizarre or unprofessional on camera, so it's important to assess our performances regularly and objectively, hence the exercises included in this course.

You may find having a monitor of what the camera is capturing facing you as you present to be distracting, or you may find that instant feedback of seeing yourself perform helps you. It's useful to write down our mistakes as we see them on playback and try to make a mental note of them for next time.

Try recreating your tics and bad habits in your day to day and cultivate an awareness of how they physically feel. The next step is to nurture a mindfulness of your physical being on camera, and once you feel the tic or twitch manifesting, arrest it on the fly.

If you lean your head, some people will find keeping it stock still helps with losing the habit. Others may find that using more head movement, to even it out, fixes the problem. Because the problem is unique to you, sometimes the solution can be too.

If you gesticulate wildly, try holding your hands in an open neutral position in front of you, then practice using the gestures from this course mindfully. If sitting presenting from a desk, you can hold one thumb inside your other hand, to control nervous twitches, or rest your hands on your lap. Another option is to take a prop like a mic or clipboard, to arrest excessive hand movement.

Shifting uncomfortably is another habit to avoid, so I always recommend presenters and guests 'anchor in' as described in our section on posture.

Because everybody is different, there's no one size fits all solution to this, but if watching yourself back and consistent practice isn't fixing the issue, you can try working with a coach to help arrest bad habits and impulses over time. Mostly this should come with practice, however, so remember to watch yourself back objectively, consistently, take notes, and try to iron out bad habits gradually over time.

Exercise 10. Pulling it all Together Part 2

Now it's time to put everything you've learned into practice. You're going to do three new videos. Do them all in a row, so you're nice and relaxed and warmed up for the last one.

1. The first video is another run-through of the sample script, which you should know quite well by now. Warm up first, with both body and vocal exercises. Calm yourself with square breathing if nervous. Check your gesture plan and breathing strategies. Print out or load up your script on a prompt, and present into camera (or as close to camera as you can with the script pinned next to it).
2. Now you're going to do another improvised video to camera, unscripted. Do this straight after the other video, and into the lens. Talk about yourself, your work, your interests, and what you hope to bring to the camera.
3. Last one. This time, you'll follow this video with a completely improvised piece. Talk for three minutes on any subject that takes your fancy (your specialist subject is usually best, but it can be anything you love). Time yourself and wrap it up as practised in 'Talking to Time' when the timer goes off.

Now take the Self-Evaluation Checklist and evaluate all three performances, noting your strengths and weaknesses. Be sure to concentrate on shoring up your weaknesses and exploiting your strengths as much as possible.

Congratulations! You're well on your way to giving smooth, confident, authoritative presentations!

Bonus Chapter: Self-Shooting

It's becoming increasingly common to film our own content as technology and online distribution becomes more widely available. There are a host of options in order to do this, and whilst recommending specific techniques, equipment and setting up a professional studio are outside the remit of this book, let's look at some basics, in the event you want to experiment with content creation from scratch.

Setting

This can be the 'make or break' for many a budding self-shooter. Where you decide to shoot will affect how your video looks, how your audience perceives you, and the level of professionalism your video can reach. The 'simple white background' popularised by companies like Apple is deceptively hard to achieve, and without adequate lighting (see below) it's far more likely to look like a 'dirty grey background', and worse than simply shooting at your bedroom desk. It's becoming increasingly common for self-shooters to shoot at home, and we as viewers are becoming more used to seeing domestic settings onscreen. If you're going to shoot at home, be mindful of what is in the background. Choose an area which won't have people or animals walking in the background, as this is highly distracting (although intentionally including pets in videos is extremely popular).

Curate your backdrop. A backdrop is anything that can be seen on screen. You want your backdrop to message-match the type of video you're putting out. Don't have clutter if you're talking about tidying and organisation, for example. If you shoot about a niche sub-culture, then it's probably visually interesting for your viewers to see lots of items related to that culture in the backdrop. Just think about curating the right visual vocabulary for your branding and target audience.

A common backdrop is a wall of suitable books, a couch with appropriate art on the wall, or simply a well-lit tidy room (a little greenery never hurts, either). Something to bear in mind is that everything looks messier on camera. The camera has a way of picking out every little thing and making it stand out. Cat toy left on the floor? Congratulations, now your potential viewer is obsessed with working out what that is. It can be frustrating trying to set up a 'studio-look' at home – many of us don't have a perfectly sized blank wall and adequate lighting (see below) to make that work. When you start off, try not to over-think it, and just make a bespoke setting with a backdrop you're comfortable with. Be sure to remove any embarrassing items from your backdrop, shoot a test run, and watch it back. You'll know what you want to change once you see it on screen.

Framing

Framing describes the position of the subject(s) on screen relative to the borders, or frame. Because the camera determines how the viewer perceives us, using framing effectively can confer tone and even on-screen authority, so it's important to get right. The tone of a piece can be thought of as the way you want the audience to feel. If you want an intimate, friendly tone, you may want to frame in close-up. For a demonstration, you'll want to frame so that whatever you're showing off can be seen (including objects or a blackboard, backdrop etc.).

When considering framing, it can help to think of your camera as the viewer. What do you want them to see? How do you want them to perceive you? If you're using a prompt, as described later, you'll likely need to keep the camera at eye-level, as you'll want to be able to look directly into the camera. However, some self-shooters and YouTubers use framing to great effect, even when shooting with a mobile phone. Perhaps they place the camera low, in order to capture a building or natural phenomenon behind them. However, be mindful that placing the camera low means that you're literally talking 'down' to the viewer. Sometimes, if done subtly this can confer authority, but it generally isn't a flattering angle and wouldn't normally be recommended for a piece to camera. Generally, you want to make sure that all your head (or at least face, for a close-up) is in in shot, and leave a margin of space around you to allow for movement. Many self-shooters place themselves into the middle of the frame, leaving a little space (about a hands-width) above the top of their heads, and just go by eye, using their best guess. This is usually fine, and there's no need to over complicate self-shooting, but if you want some more specific guidance on framing, you can use the rule of thirds.

The Rule of Thirds

It is standard practice in the film industry to imagine the frame as split into three equal parts horizontally and three equal parts vertically, leaving us with a nine square 'grid' of roughly equal parts. The intersections of these lines create four points of crossover, creating a smaller imaginary box in the middle our frame. These four central intersecting points are pleasing to the eye, and as such, when you look at the framing of most major motion pictures, you'll notice that the subject is often placed at one of these points. The top horizontal line is useful when gauging where your eyeline should be when directly addressing the camera. The first and third vertical lines are where we place the subject if we want it off-centre. This is a creative choice. Many 'to camera' pieces are shot from the middle of the screen, and this is fine. However, you can film a piece to camera from one of these thirds if you want to create something visually interesting, or if you're showing something else large on screen (if you were talking about a painting or statue, or vehicle for example).

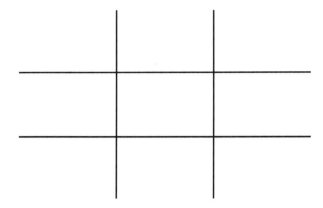

Imagine this grid overlay on your screen when you picture using thirds. The four points where the lines intersect are where subjects are typically placed. The top line is a good guide for eyeline.

Lead Room/Nose Room

If you do decide to shoot using thirds there's one more consideration to make and that's lead room. Sometimes called 'nose room' because it refers to leaving space on the screen in the direction you're facing. So, if you place the subject (including yourself) on the right side of the screen, and you decide to use angles, then you need to be angled or facing left. Somebody on the left would be angled right. This is due to the visual illusion that makes it look strange if you're facing the same side of the edge that you're closest to. Please note that you can employ thirds for a straight to camera piece without any angles or profiles, and discard nose room. Lead room, or nose room only comes into play when you can see a profile or facing.

Choosing a Camera Type

Shooting video with a camera isn't as difficult as it once might have been. Technology has moved so quickly in this area, that many self-shooters are packing up their professional cameras and switching out to mobile phone cameras.

DSLR
There are advantages to shooting with a digital camera, often called a DSLR. You can switch out the lens to better suit the size of the room, shot and framing, and you often have more control over focus, aperture and exposure. Don't worry if these all sound like intimidating technical jargon terms, there are many guides and videos online to help you get a grip on handling a DSLR.

The pros of a DSLR are many. You will have high quality footage, usually recorded straight to a memory card which you can then transfer to a computer and edit as desired. You can choose a camera and lens that allows for maximum customisation of shots, meaning you get to play with cool effects such as Depth of Field and what cinematographers call 'bokeh.' Bokeh is an effect used often but rarely explained, and simply describes the process of having a close-up subject in focus and leaving the background blurry. This makes the subject look crisper, and, using simple lights for effect, can make the background look far more attractive.

The cons of a DSLR are initial cost and time to master. Not only will a decent DSLR set you back many hundreds, sometimes thousands of pounds, but you also need lenses, memory cards, tripods, and occasionally other peripherals. You can rarely if ever edit on a camera, so you'll need a computer and software in order to do that.

Given that you have so much more control, such cameras come with a steeper learning curve. It takes time to master things like aperture, ISO and shutter speed. Again, there are many videos and tutorials out there, so if you're technically-minded and want to create your own beautifully bokeh custom content, this could be an option for you – just don't get so obsessed with how the video looks that you let it put you off getting content out there!

But if you don't know your F-Stops from your bus stops, don't panic. You can make a perfectly serviceable video with just a phone or webcam.

Phones and Webcams

The advantage of phone video recording is that almost everybody has access to a mobile phone these days, and the cameras on phones are becoming good enough to give low-end (and even some higher-end) DSLRs a run for their money. Similarly, there are enough high-definition webcams available at affordable prices that it's becoming less common to need a professional camera, especially if you only shoot at home. There are a few things to bear in mind when shooting with a phone or webcam, and these considerations can apply whatever device you're shooting on.

- Definition/Resolution – most videos online are available at 720p and 1080p. It's possible to go higher definition than this, but I'd advise against this when starting out. Remember that the higher the resolution of your recording, the more storage space it requires, and the more memory you'll need available when editing it. Check what resolution your phone, camera or webcam records in so that you're not caught out when trying to upload it.
- Always check the recommended settings and format of the site you hope to host content on. Some will accept multiple formats and resolutions, others will be more specific. Never assume, and always makes sure you're shooting in the right specs.
- Aspect – Unless specifically stated otherwise, always shoot in landscape mode (if recording with a phone, it will usually need to be on its side). It's amazing how many videos I see of professionals self-shooting with their cameras in portrait mode. This creates ugly black bars at the side of the screen when you upload and shrinks your picture down, so shoot in landscape to make the most of that widescreen aspect and resolution.

- Uploads – If you're uploading content from a camera, you need a memory card reader to transfer to a pc. If you're shooting from a phone and want to edit on a pc make sure you can access your phone's memory in order to transfer footage.

Overall, using a phone or webcam is an inexpensive way to get shooting and creating content, and highly recommended for people starting out, and those looking to streamline the process. Additionally, if shooting on a phone or using mobile apps, many sites now have native editors, saving you the time and cost of learning editing. If you want to record audio with the phone, make sure it has an audio input and not just an on-board microphone (see below).

There are apps for scrolling text on phone screens and desktops if you want a makeshift prompt machine for your videos, but equally if you prefer to riff, just create a list of talking points!

Lighting

Let's begin with one hard rule: never rely on domestic lighting when you shoot video. A camera requires far more available light than the eye and using the regular lights we use at home on video generally looks terrible. You also have no control over the *intensity* and *direction* of the light, both of which are key to lighting a subject (you) and backdrop. Domestic lighting tends to swing between too scattered and dark, and too harsh (i.e bright overhead lighting on a subject). It's also often completely the wrong tone and makes it harder for your camera to do something we call a 'white-balance,' leaving the screen looking quite jaundiced. If you're going to the effort of learning to present well, don't be let down by lighting when self-shooting!

Thankfully there are a host of lighting options available on the market from the affordable to the professional. Budget options aren't always noticeably worse, especially if you're only shooting at your desktop, and will make a visible difference on screen.

When navigating lighting you'll likely come across a bewildering range of accessories, terminology and advice. Don't be intimidated by all this. Just learn the basics, experiment, and learn what works for you.

Lighting Setup

Lighting is a complex field, both a science and an art. I'm by no means a master of lighting, and teaching it is somewhat outside the scope of this book. However, I've run enough shoots to appreciate how important it is and advise at least the following.

You will often need at least two lights, designed specifically for filming or photography. Each light is usually placed roughly in line with the camera and angled towards the subject at approx. 30-45 degrees. This helps light the face evenly whilst giving you options to accentuate or downplay certain features. If you only light one side of the face, or only light face-on, it can cast strange shadows and hard lines that look odd on camera (depending on the light type, see below). Employing two lights at opposing angles gives you greater control, softening this effect without washing out your features.

In addition, when setting up a studio type shoot, it's common to place two additional lights roughly in line with the presenter (off-camera) in order to light the background. A well-lit subject on a dark background can work if done stylistically, but often it simply looks flat. Lighting the background brings out the colour and detail of the set and is often the reason a professionally shot video looks so much clearer and cleaner than an amateur video.

Finally, it's sometimes recommended to have a 'hair' or 'rim' light. This is a light which sit directly above the head facing down on the subject. It lights the top of the head (hence 'hair' light) and helps separate the subject from the background. This is often a more difficult light to set up, as it often needs to hang on a clamped stand which must be counter-weighted or balanced.

If all this sounds a little bit much: -

Soft Boxes

'Soft Boxes' look more like traditional photography set lighting composing a stand topped by a collapsible 'lamp-shade' style box with cradles for 1-5 light globes (bulbs). These are typical of photography shoots and often sell under that banner. These lights are often ideal if you plan to present whilst standing, as they are self-supporting and tall enough to light the head and face. The downside is that they require space and often aren't dimmable. As such you can only change the intensity of light by vicinity to the subject, or by increasing/decreasing the number of physical lights. When I shot my presenting video course, I started the shoot with two soft box lights. By the time I was on reshoots I owned five, so bear in mind that this isn't always the most affordable way to start. Lighting on stands are also not practical for shooting at a desk, as there isn't enough distance to diffuse the light properly and the base takes a lot of space. That said, there are plenty of good quality soft boxes available online ranging from around £50 a pair at time of writing.

LED Lighting

There are increasing numbers of lighting rigs which attach to a phone or camera and light the face directly. These range from square LED panels to lightweight rings of tiny LED bulbs. Often adjustable so that you can control the intensity and tone/colour of the light, LED boards are often an affordable, lightweight option for the self-shooter. If you plan to present on the move, on location, or simply want to keep lighting minimal, these are an excellent option when starting out. There are plenty of buyers guides online to find the LED panel that suits your needs, just remember to keep a selection of batteries available if you don't have mains power at location.

Diffusers and Gels

These are simply transparent or semi-transparent heat-resistant plastics or materials used to cover a light and diffuse the intensity by scattering the light or change its tone by altering the colour. If you find the lighting on your videos too intense or harsh, consider using a diffuser. If you find the tone too cold, use a warm-toned gel. Too warm? Use a cool (often blue) gel. Again, experiment, find your look, and with it your unique style and brand will develop.

Audio/Sound

Audio is one of the most important aspects of shooting to get right. Your video could look like a million dollars, but if the sound is poor, echoey, tinny, or worse, painful, nobody is going to watch it. As with lighting, the difference between a video with good and bad audio can be the difference between appearing professional or amateur.

The good news is that sound equipment is cheap, widely available, and generally very easy to use, so there's no excuse to let your videos sound as if they were shot on a bridge in high winds!

Remember to position your mic where it can pick up your voice easily but don't place it so close that it peaks or pops. This effect is what happens when we expose the mic to too much volume and it cannot process it, resulting in unusable sound. Always use pop shields if they aren't built-in. These are the fuzzy or foamy black covers your typically 'sheath' over the mic head. Make sure lapel-attached 'lav' mics (see below) are in place and turned on, check everything is plugged in, then monitor the sound levels as you record. Do not bash or tap the mic and try to avoid rustling the mic with your movements if you're wearing one ('mic'd up'). Be sure to sound check and adjust input levels accordingly. Also be sure to check the desired audio quality of your hosting site, and whether they support mono or stereo. Generally, it is advisable to record talking-head and interview pieces in *mono not stereo*. This is because you want people to be able to hear both sides of a conversation in each ear, rather than baffling them with a constantly moving audio.

There are two main things to consider when choosing how to record audio – the format you'll record on; PC, Handheld, Remote, or Phone – and following this, the type of microphone required.

PC

Recording sound to a PC is ideal if you're shooting primarily at your desk and sitting in one place. A big advantage is that most capture software (including communication software like Skype and free capture software like OBS) allows you to select the source of your microphone, so you don't have to use the (often sub-par) on board webcam mic. This gives you a great range of options from the budget to the hi-fidelity.

Portable Recorder

Portable audio recorders have come a long way from the cassette decks of the 1980s and the handheld devices of the 1990s. Today's portable devices record digitally and hold space for hours and hours of audio, depending on memory card and audio quality settings. Whilst they still often have native on-board microphones it's recommended that you invest in a suitable microphone for such a device, such as small lapel 'lav' mics. Some recorders have inputs for up to 6 microphones, but if you're starting out and only need one or two, you can get adapters for single input units. Check compatibility, as you may require adapters depending on the audio set-up and number of mics.

Remote

Remote devices tend to be wireless units, which are most often used with a receiver plugged into a camera. The microphone itself (usually a lav mic) plugs into a unit clipped to your belt, and transmits to the camera, syncing audio to your video. This is a good time to highlight that the audio on most cameras, even good DSLRs is often very poor, and used only to sync up the sound with a better recording in post-production.

Phone

As with portable recorders, if you're shooting with your phone you don't necessarily need a mic, but it is recommended. Phones, like all exposed omni-directional mics, pick up a great deal of background noise, and don't preserve the quality or depth of ambient audio. However, small lav mics for mobile phones are increasingly common, often cheap, and highly recommended for most self-shooting purposes. Lav mics are small and portable, so are an obvious solution to achieving studio-quality sound in a portable form, perfect for shooting on the move. As always, check compatibility between mic and phone inputs.

Microphones

As noted, your choice of microphone, or simply 'mic', will largely be determined by the format that you choose to record in. When choosing your format and mic, bear in mind factors such as quality, portability and general versatility (does it require a pc, or can it plug into a recorder or phone?).

USB Mics
If you're shooting at your desk or computer, these are a good option. Entry level USB mics come in a variety of shapes, sizes, and qualities. Remember to buy a stand if you get a traditionally shaped mic (unless you want to hold it and look like a 1990s news reporter). There are several USB mics in the £30-£60 price range at time of writing, and free-standing desk mics are becoming an affordable standard. There are higher-end options if you want the best sound available, but for online content this isn't usually required. The downside is that USB mics aren't typically portable and require a pc or laptop for power and audio connection.

Lavalier (Lav) Mics
Lav mics are mentioned above so many times for a reason. They're often the self-shooter's best friend being light, adaptable and capable of great quality recording in multiple environments. Lav mics are the tiny microphones you see fitted to a jacket lapel on television, often covered with a mini wind shield (always use a wind or pop shield with lav mics!). I've used lav mics everywhere from professional sets to

interviews in the street, to last-minute multiple person interviews in a dining room... with great results! For my money, the lav mic is the unsung hero of most shoots. There are many options at the low-end of the market, some are good quality, and some are too fragile for purpose. Check reviews, shop around, and as always, make sure they're compatible with your recorder.

Special Mention: Boom Mics

You've seen them on film sets, and probably seen them stray into frame on amateur productions; boom mics are the film-set standard but are used far less frequently in factual television. As a self-shooter, boom mics do not come recommended for one simple reason – they require a boom stand, and often an operator! Add in the expensive nature of the boom and accompanying equipment and you can probably see why I wouldn't rush out to buy one when you're starting your filming career.

Editing

There are several options for video editing ranging from top-end solutions like Adobe Premier Pro and Final Cut to premium freeware such as DaVinci Resolve. As mentioned, many video hosting sites have native video editing available through your browser, and mobile devices now pack enough power to edit effectively through a native app. Coming from a studio background I first learned Adobe, and miss the functionality when I use anything else, but there's much to be said for keeping it simple. Many new self-shooters over-edit and over perfect their work (I still fight the urge to do this, myself). What we forget is that viewers are used to occasional slips and fluffs, and we don't need to catch every single 'ummm' (Ideally, we won't be making that many to begin with, if we practice regularly). Editing is becoming increasingly accessible, so don't be intimidated by the range of options out there. If you're starting out, a mobile or browser app should do just fine, and as you progress you can re-evaluate whether you want to invest time and money into editing suites. If you want to place a logo on your videos, it's usually at this stage that you would do that.

Green Screens

Another technology which has become widely available at a fraction of its former price is the 'Green Screen.' I've only ever used these in professional studios, but it's become relatively simple to buy a green backdrop and suitable stands. You place this 'screen' behind you, so it covers the entire backdrop with one colour. You can then select or 'key' out the background colour in your editing suit in order to place yourself in any setting imaginable. If you want to do this your lighting needs to be excellent, and you mustn't wear or hold any items that match the background colour, lest they disappear into scenery. You also need good editing software, or a good editor, to pull this off, so I wouldn't necessarily recommend this when first starting out, but know it is an affordable option when you're ready to step up your game. The advantage is that when done well, you can place yourself on any backdrop, customise your branding by presenting in front of a virtual logo for example, and are only limited by your imagination.

Keep It Simple, Stupid (KISS)

KISS is an oft heard acronym on film sets and productions. With the vast range of post-production options available, it can be tempting to throw everything at a video, but this isn't always the best route. Try not to become too distracted by the technology, and certainly don't let gimmicks get in the way of your story. Repetitive stylistic cuts and transitions may look impressive at first but can quickly become distracting or tiresome. Focus on a clean, simple style whilst you master your content, and worry about adding flourish later. A little goes a long way, and techy gimmicks should be the seasoning, not the main course.

Also remember that as a self-shooter you must fill multiple roles. You are your producer, director, sound tech, lights and director of photography! Don't let this scare you off the process...it's all extremely manageable with practice, but it's worth highlighting how many areas you need to consider when creating quality content.

Additionally, as your own director, you need to set your tone, keep energy high, and be your own worst critic when watching material back.

Bringing energy to a piece and setting tone can be challenging, so find a level which works for you. A conversational tone is usually well-received on most platforms, and as with dealing with the camera in previous chapters, addressing your webcam or phone as a friend is often a solid approach. Just remember to look into the camera, and not off-screen too much, as this can make you look disinterested. Treat your home, or location self-shoots as if they're pro shoots, and eventually, they will become so!

Final Thoughts

You've finished the book, but your journey may be just beginning. Don't forget to practice the exercises included, until you yearn for something more challenging! You can up the stakes by changing the timing of the piece (longer presentations are much harder to shoot in one take), adding links, and walking on and off camera. Keep filming and challenging yourself and try to shoot a new video at least twice a week if you can. You don't need to do anything complex, just practice getting the key techniques down, such as posture and breathing, and work on the technical stuff at your own pace! I've included a self-evaluation form for you to revisit your videos and keep track of your progress.

Be patient with yourself as frustration and perfectionism won't help create a good performance. If you make a mistake just breathe deep and keep practising. You will get the hang of it.

Appendices

1. Self-Evaluation Sheet

1. Preparation
- Did you do any vocal warmups? How did they affect your voice?
- Did you do any breathing exercises to relax prior to recording?
- How about power poses?
- If you compare your performance post-warmup to your original 'control' video, how do they measure up?

2. Breathing
- Where are you breathing from? Stomach or chest? (Always aim for lower abdomen!)
- Are you taking deep breaths or multiple shallow breaths?
- How did you handle your breathing? Were you strategic, or did you just muddle through?
- How could you improve your breathing strategy and where could you build in pauses for breath in the script?

3. Confidence
- Does your body language imply confidence or nervousness?
- What about posture?
- Does your voice waver, or is it strong and authoritative?

- How does your breathing affect your voice, and in turn, your air of authority?
- What kind of presence do you have? Is it –
1. Authoritative?
2. Calm?
3. Charming?
4. Commanding?
5. Endearing?
6. Energetic?
7. Funny?
8. High Impact?
9. Inspiring?
10. Knowledgeable?
11. Nervous?
12. Passionate?
13. Sagely and wise?

All of these are fine, as even nerves can help bring energy to a piece. Just be sure to avoid the following –
1. Angry
2. Apathetic
3. Arrogant
4. Boring
5. Dull
6. Indifferent
7. Morose
8. Scared
9. Shy
10. Shrill

11. Quiet

- Unless these are specific personas you're bringing to screen for parodic or dramatic purposes, of course!

4. Diction
- Are your words clear and understandable?
- Did you stumble on certain words?
- When you stumble, do you return to the top of the sentence, the paragraph, or lose your flow completely?
- How was your delivery speed compared to your control video?

5. Expression
- Did you fix your camera face before the take began?
- Do your expressions match the tone of the piece?
- When you smile, does it seem sincere or forced?
- How can you bring more genuine emotion to expressions?
- Do your expressions match the framing and size of the piece?

6. Eyeline
- Does eyeline match the lens?
- Do you keep your eyes on the lens throughout?
- If not, why not? Are you co-presenting, or demonstrating an object?

- Does your gaze wander? How does this affect your connection with the viewer and command of their attention?

7. Gestures
- Are your gestures strategic, or nervous tics?
- Are you message matching?
- Did you use a gesture strategy, or have a few gestures planned for certain parts?
- Did you use The Give, The Show, or The Point?
- Where did you hold your hands when not gesturing?

8. Intonation
- Do you sound convincingly conversational?
- Does your voice rise and fall in pitch (good modulation), or are you monotone?

9. Posture
- Is there space built into your body?
- Are you slouching?
- How can you better support your upper body and head?
- Is your head over your shoulders or protruding forward?

- Are you 'open' or is your body closed off?
- Can you maintain your on-camera posture for extended periods comfortably?
- How does posture affect breathing, vocal power, confidence, and authority?

10. Prompts
- What prompt speed did you find most comfortable?
- Do you sound like you're reading? If so, aim for more conversational tone.
- Is your eyeline in the middle of the screen?
- Do your eyes flicker too much over the text? Do they move too much from the top of the page to the bottom?
- Is it obvious that you're reading? If so, move the prompt (and camera) further back and reframe.
- Are you planning your breathing according to breaks in the script?
- How is diction and pronunciation?

11. Scripts
- Do you write in long or short sentences?
- Are your scripts full of jargon? Can the average viewer relate?
- Did you proof read your script aloud?
- Did your script match the intended time of the video?
- Do you think you'd benefit from putting in more or fewer spaces between lines or paragraphs?

- How was tone and intonation? How was use of gesture? How would you make a gesture plan for this and other scripts?

12. General
- Did you seem natural and relaxed or tense?
- Do you seem sincere and relatable?
- Do you feel you're connecting to the audience?
- Would you watch you? What about your performance might make you switch channel? (We almost all have something we'd change).
- What about your performance would keep you watching?

2. Sample Script

Hello, I'm (your name).

The term, 'Cleopatra's Needle' is actually a misnomer. It's an Egyptian obelisk from the reign of Tuthmose III. This is what we call a cartouche and it holds one of the names of the king...
(indicates cartouche)
...in this case Men-Khefe-Ra. He reigned 1,000 years before any Cleopatra reigned in Egypt. This was also 3,000 years before the needle came to rest on London's embankment. The history of the needle is quite remarkable. It was originally one of a pair erected at the entrance to the Temple of the Sun in the ancient city of Heliopolis near Cairo. It stood there for over a thousand years but was overturned during an invasion by the Persians in the fifth century BCE.

500 years later, it was resurrected, and placed outside a temple dedicated to Julius Caesar in Alexandria, where it stood for thirteen centuries! It toppled in a major earthquake but was once again excavated in the early 1800s. The needle became a gift presented to Great Britain in 1819 by the ruler of Egypt, Mohamed Ali.

Not including (your name), this script is 178 words long, or just under a minute at three words per-second (ideal delivery speed). However, I intentionally selected a piece which contained multiple long words and difficult pronunciations. If you can get through this piece without stumbling, most pieces should be a breeze.

Printed in Poland
by Amazon Fulfillment
Poland Sp. z o.o., Wrocław